BACKYARD BBQ

BACKYARD

BBQ

DELICIOUS RECIPES FOR OUTDOOR COOKING

MARCUS BAWDON

DOG 'n' BONE

Published in 2025 by Dog 'n' Bone Books
an imprint of Ryland Peters & Small
20–21 Jockey's Fields, London WC1R 4BW
and
1452 Davis Bugg Road, Warrenton, NC 27589

www.rylandpeters.com

10 9 8 7 6 5 4 3 2 1

A CIP catalogue record for this book is
available from the British Library.

ISBN: 978-1-912983-84-1

Printed in China

Designer: Alison Fenton
Food Photography & Styling: Marcus Bawdon
Copy Editor: Kate Eddison
Editorial Director: Julia Charles
Head of Production Patricia Harrington
Art Director: Sally Powell
Creative Director: Leslie Harrington

IMPORTANT SAFETY NOTES
* Keep raw meat, poultry, fish and their juices
away from other food. After cutting raw meats,
wash boards, utensils and countertops with
hot, soapy water. These can be sanitzied by
using a solution of 1 tbsp of unscented, liquid
chlorine bleach in 4.5 litres/1 gallon of water.

* Take care whenever you are cooking with live
fire, remember that any nearby surfaces will get
hot, sparks can fly, and hot liquid and fat may
spill onto your skin. Always have a first-aid kit,
as well as a fire extinguisher and fire blanket,
close to where you are cooking. ALWAYS
supervise children, near a barbecue or fire.

MIX
Paper | Supporting
responsible forestry
FSC® C008047

CONTENTS

INTRODUCTION

IF YOU ARE NEAR A FIRE, YOU CAN COOK!

Barbecuing is a primal technique for cooking food; there is often nothing simpler. You don't always need fancy gadgets, just food and fire. By cooking directly in the embers of a fire, you take the simplest of foods and turn them into something special. You only need good embers, quality lumpwood charcoal, or the embers of a hardwood or fruitwood fire. You can then simply place the food straight in the embers… That's it. Here, I look at the simplest of barbecue techniques that use a minimal amount of kit, meaning anyone can achieve delicious results.

I love cooking in this way and I am massively inspired by proponents of this style, such as chefs Francis Mallmann, Adam Perry Lang, and Niklas Ekstedt. For certain ingredients there is no better way of cooking them – the exposure to direct heat caramelizes food like no other way. It is also a way of life – to appreciate food cooked outdoors, to experience lots of big bold flavours, to use your hands to eat, and to enjoy life to the full.

I grew up in front of the fire. On cold nights, my large family would sit in front of the flames and together we would cook honest, simple food in the embers of the fire. Jacket potatoes with charred crisp skin were the family favourite, a slab of butter melting into the middle. Toasting chestnuts in the embers was another prized activity and these taste memories are locked into my soul now. I then started to work in many far-flung places, where I was exposed to new food cultures. I travelled extensively and learned to cook many new styles, constantly expanding my flavour palate.

Visits to Morocco, Thailand, India and Africa all had a huge influence on me.

When I moved to a house in rural Devon, I started to cook more and more: campfires, smokers and wood-fired ovens all started to appear in my garden. This interest quickly grew into an all-consuming passion – I never tire of delving into the world of food and fire, serving up exciting creations inspired by grilling cultures around the world. I love to show people what is possible with flame and to explain how to cook on anything from simple fire pits to hi-tech pellet grills. This led me to run a Facebook Group – CountryWoodSmoke – where people learn and share various artisanal techniques, from bacon curing to bread making. Alongside this I run the UK BBQ School, where I teach everyone from beginners to chefs looking to learn new skills. I also regularly host and demonstrate at live outdoor cooking events, with whole weekends spent teaching butchery, fire control, grilling, smoking and barbecuing. I've also been a barbecue judge at Grillstock, Qfest and Pengrillie and am a Kansas City BBQ Society Certified BBQ Judge. One of my proudest own moments was being crowned King of Meatopia at the inaugural London Meatopia, one of the UK's biggest barbecue events.

For me, now, the best times are always spent in front of a fire, be it drinking whiskey round the firepit with good mates, or sitting in front of the woodstove with my children, toasting marshmallows and chestnuts. I look forward to sharing some of these moments and the passion I have for food and fire with you.

CHAPTER 1

BEEF

I have many friends from South Africa, and they are very proud of their braai culture, so I ran this recipe by a few of them to make sure it wouldn't cause any upset. Needless to say, it had unanimous approval! I was in two minds about skewering sausage, as it can easily lose its juice to the flames. I decided to use very fine skewers so the holes were minimal. Skewering maintains the shape of the sausage wheel, so it can be loaded up with the cheese and chutney (according to my friends it has to be Mrs Balls chutney, made with dried fruit and a hint of chilli for heat). I used a Namibian hardwood kameeldoring (camelthorn), which can be bought online if you want to try it.

BOEREWORS, CHEESE & CHUTNEY

FEEDS 2

RECOMMENDED HEAT
moderate

1 large boerewors sausage
in a wheel (about 500 g/
1 lb. 2 oz.)

50 g/½ packed cup plus
1 tablespoon grated Cheddar
cheese

3 tablespoons Mrs Balls Chutney,
or other spiced fruit chutney

chunky bread, to serve

very fine metal skewers

Set up your barbecue with a bed of hot charcoal – a couple of handfuls should be enough. Place two small pieces of braaiwood, such as camelthorn, on to the coals and let the wood burn down to embers. You could use oak or cherry, but it won't have the authentic flavour of braaiwood. Once the flames have settled down and you have a fragrant bed of embers (around 180°C/350°F), you are ready to start cooking.

Place two very fine metal skewers at 90 degrees to each other through the sausage to hold the shape together. Cook the sausage slowly – ideally with the lid down. It should take about 15 minutes to reach an internal temperature of 74°C/165°F on a digital probe thermometer. Top the sausage with the grated cheese and chutney, following the wheel of the sausage. Cook with the lid down for another 5 minutes or so until the cheese has melted.

Serve the sausage with chunks of bread and enjoy with a cold beer.

I first cooked a Stinking Bishop-stuffed burger many years ago, but I wanted to recreate this wonderful dish for this book. Stinking Bishop, as its name suggests, is a strong pungent cheese, but it is also very creamy and works really nicely with dry-aged beef. The cheese goes really melty and oozy.

STINKING BISHOP-STUFFED BURGERS

FEEDS 2

RECOMMENDED HEAT
moderate–high

4 thin dry-aged beef patties or 400 g/14 oz. minced/ground dry-aged beef shaped into 4 patties

60 g/2 oz. Stinking Bishop or other strong cheese, grated

1 onion, thinly sliced

15 g/1 tablespoon butter

2 brioche burger buns, toasted

2 tablespoons piccalilli

4 double-pronged metal skewers

Set up your barbecue for cooking on a hot plate or in a cast-iron pan over moderate–high heat (180–200°C/ 350–400°F).

Take two of the patties and place half of the cheese in between them. Press the patties together to seal the cheese in the middle. Repeat with the remaining patties and cheese.

Sear the burgers on the hot plate or cast-iron pan, and cook on both sides until the meat is cooked through (has reached an internal temperature of 74°C/165°F on a digital probe thermometer) and the cheese has melted. Remove and set aside.

Add the onion and butter to the hot plate or pan and cook until charred and soft.

Serve the burgers on toasted brioche buns with the charred onions and some piccalilli for a powerfully flavoured, juicy burger.

I have travelled to various Scandinavian countries with my day job over the years, and while working in Norway I tried Beef Lindstrom, a classic dish from neighbouring Sweden, which is a delicious burger patty containing chopped beetroot and capers. I really wanted to try this on my grill back home.

BEEF LINDSTROM BURGERS

FEEDS 2

RECOMMENDED HEAT
moderate

2 small beetroots/beets

2 teaspoons capers

240 g/9 oz. minced/ground beef

2 slices sourdough bread, toasted

a handful of rocket/arugula

2 tablespoons mayonnaise

1 teaspoon creamed horseradish

sea salt and freshly ground black pepper

Set up your barbecue for direct cooking over moderate heat (around 180°C/350°F).

Place the beetroots directly in the coals and cook until they are charred on the outside and soft on the inside, 25–30 minutes.

Finely chop one of the beetroots and the capers, then add to the beef and mix together. Form the mixture into two patties, then grill over direct heat until the meat is cooked through and has reached an internal temperature of 74°C/165°F on a digital probe thermometer.

Top the toasted sourdough bread with the rocket and then the patties. Mix together the mayonnaise and horseradish, and spread on top. Finally, chop the second ember-cooked beetroot and add to the top.

As much as I love a proper 'full packer' cut of brisket, sometimes I don't fancy cooking a whole one. Rolled brisket is great slow-cooked and braised in a nice liquid, such as beer! I'm a big fan of the smoke–braise–dip method: smoke until you're happy with the crust on the outside; braise in a suitable container, with a liquid such as stock, beer or wine; then dip the sliced brisket in the braising liquor when serving. Jonathan from Black Tor Brewery on the edge of Dartmoor gave me a few bottles of his ales to see what I could come up with.

BRISKET POT ROAST

SERVES 4

RECOMMENDED HEAT
low

1 red onion, thinly sliced

2 garlic cloves, thinly sliced

2 kg/4½ lb. rolled brisket

6 tablespoons beef rub (I used the wonderful Quiet Waters Farm Grass Fed Beef Rub)

500 ml/2 cups your favourite dark beer

sea salt and freshly ground black pepper

brioche rolls, to serve

Set up your barbecue for indirect cooking over low heat (around 130°C/265°F) with the lid on, adding a few chunks of cherry and pecan wood to smoke on the coals for additional flavour and colour.

Place the onion and garlic in a small baking pan and place the brisket on top. Season the meat with the beef rub, then smoke the brisket on the barbecue with the lid on for 5 hours.

After 5 hours, pour half the beer over the brisket – enjoy the other half as a 'pit boss perk' – and then wrap the baking pan snugly with foil.

Cook for a further 4 hours at 130°C/265°F until the internal temperature of the brisket reaches 96°C/205°F on a digital probe thermometer and the meat is soft like butter when probed.

Remove from the barbecue, cover the pan with foil, and let rest for 30 minutes in the braising liquor. Season the liquor with salt and pepper to taste.

Cut the meat into thick slices, fill the brioche rolls and serve with the braising liquor for dunking.

In my day job in the oil industry I have been fortunate to travel to some really interesting places. I worked in Nigeria for a couple of years in the late 90s and vividly remember piles of suya – beef in a spicy peanut rub – being cooked over charcoal on large grills. Many years later, in the cooler climate of Aberdeen, I cooked suya on a charcoal grill for a friend, who liked these skewers nice and crispy. I use peanut butter powder in the rub, which is pretty easy to obtain, but feel free to use pre-made suya powder if you can get it from an African shop.

SUYA

FEEDS 2

RECOMMENDED HEAT
high

500 g/1 lb. 2 oz. hanger steak (or rump steak)

3½ tablespoons rapeseed/canola oil

SUYA RUB

40 g/1½ oz. peanut butter powder

½ teaspoon cayenne pepper

1 teaspoon fine sea salt

1 teaspoon onion powder

1 teaspoon garlic granules

½ teaspoon finely ground black pepper

pre-soaked long wooden skewers

Set up your barbecue for close proximity direct grilling over high heat (around 200°C/400°F). You want hot embers with a little flame left in them.

Ensure the steaks are trimmed and any sinew removed (they sometimes have a length of tough sinew going down the middle between the two lobes of steak – ask your butcher to remove it if it's still there, or cut it out using a sharp knife). Cut the steak across the grain into long slices about the thickness of your finger and thread on to the skewers. Drizzle over the oil and rub it into the meat.

To make the suya rub, in a bowl mix together all the ingredients until combined. Sprinkle evenly over the steak.

Cook for about 3 minutes on each side until cooked to your liking. I prefer my steak to be medium–rare (with an internal temperature of 55°C/130°F on a digital probe thermometer), but I know many might prefer things a little more well done and crispy.

Serve immediately, hot off the grill.

The simple way is often the best. These skewers are made with just three ingredients, but are wonderfully tasty. The key is really good beef (around 20 per cent fat) that has been twice ground through a medium plate on a mincer to get the right texture – a good butcher should be able to do this for you. Chuck is a great cut for this, or ask your butcher for their fatty burger mince. These are great served in a hot dog bun with cheese on top.

SWEET SMOKY BEEF SKEWERS

FEEDS 4

**RECOMMENDED HEAT
high**

600 g/1 lb. 5 oz. minced/
ground beef (20% fat)

3 tablespoons barbecue dry
rub of your choice

5 tablespoons barbecue
sauce of your choice

hot dog buns and grated
Cheddar cheese, to serve
(optional)

wide, flat metal skewers

Set up your barbecue for direct grilling over high heat (around 200°C/400°F).

Use your hands to mould the minced beef on to your skewers, so it covers three-quarters of the length of the skewer. It should be around 2 cm/¾ inch thick and no more (if it's too thick it will be heavy and the meat will simply slide off the skewer).

Dust the beef with a little of the dry rub, making sure it's evenly covered.

Place the skewers on the grill and cook for 4–5 minutes on each side until brown.

Brush on the barbecue sauce and finish off the skewers for a minute or so on each side – make sure the sauce doesn't burn and the internal temperature of the meat has reached 74°C/165°F on a digital probe thermometer.

Serve in a hot dog bun topped with grated cheese, if liked.

I always enjoy visiting my local butcher, especially when he has something a bit special to try. This time, it was some Aberdeen Angus tomahawk steaks that had been dry-aged for at least 50 days – I knew I had to taste them. These are essentially the ribeye steak 'côte de boeuf' with the full rib bone trimmed and kept long. This is the pinnacle of big joints of dry-aged beef, which I like to cook straight on the coals, 'dirty' style. It's so simple and I really urge you to give this method of cooking a go. The meat develops really deep flavours that will blow you away. Trust me, you will never look back.

DIRTY TOMAHAWK STEAK

FEEDS 2–4

RECOMMENDED HEAT
moderate–high

2 tomahawk steaks, each about 900 g/2 lb.

green salad, vegetables of your choice, rice and crusty sourdough, to serve (optional)

BASTE

2 garlic cloves

3 sprigs rosemary

3 sprigs thyme

3 sprigs flat-leaf parsley

3 tablespoons coarse rock salt

6 tablespoons olive oil

squeeze of lemon juice

Set up your barbecue with good-quality lump charcoal and get the coals nice and hot. Wait for the flames to die down before cooking the steaks.

First, make the baste by blitzing all the ingredients in a food processor or using a hand blender until you have a bright green paste.

Brush each steak with some baste and place each one directly on the coals. Cook for a few minutes on each side, basting every now and again.

Move the steaks to one side of the grill to smoke with the barbecue lid down for 20 minutes until they reach the desired internal temperature of 46°C/115°F on a digital probe thermometer. Remove from the coals and rest for 10 minutes.

Cut the steaks into thin slices, and serve with a green salad, vegetables, rice and crusty sourdough, if you like.

Steak and mushrooms are a classic combination on the barbecue, and here I've given them an oriental twist, using finest fillet steak and enoki mushrooms, which are often used in Japanese cuisine. These unusual mushrooms are too delicate to be grilled directly by themselves, but wrapping them in thin slivers of fillet steak protects them a little. Brushed with a hit of savoury teriyaki sauce, this wonderfully simple recipe will certainly impress.

FILLET STEAK & ENOKI SKEWERS

FEEDS 4 starter or side

RECOMMENDED HEAT
high

500 g/1 lb. 2 oz. fillet steak

250 g/9 oz. enoki mushrooms

6 tablespoons teriyaki sauce, plus extra for dipping

sea salt and freshly ground black pepper

sushi rice, to serve (optional)

flat metal skewers

Set up your barbecue for direct cooking over high heat (around 200°C/400°F), with the coals close to the grill grates for close proximity grilling.

Using a sharp knife, slice the fillet steak into very thin slices across the grain, as thin as you can manage.

Break the enoki mushrooms into little groups of 8–10; a little of the base can be included in each group to keep it intact. Place each group of mushrooms on a slice of steak and roll up so the mushrooms are wrapped up snugly.

Carefully thread 2 or 3 onto each metal skewer. Season the parcels with salt and freshly ground pepper, then brush on a little of the teriyaki sauce.

Grill over high heat for 2–3 minutes on each side. The fillet steak should be slightly charred, as should the mushrooms.

Serve with some sushi rice, if you like, and a little extra teriyaki sauce for dipping.

Ever since I first had a play with a wood-fired oven, I'd wanted to cook a nice steak in one. My wife loves steak fajitas, so, of course, I wanted to come up with a recipe she would love. I had a lovely piece of skirt steak, which proved perfect for these fajitas. I cooked the steak in a pellet-powered wood-fired oven, which can reach up to 400°C/750°F in under 20 minutes, and used a cast-iron steak sizzler pan. This dish has a fantastic flavour – the mocha rub, with its hints of coffee, chocolate, cumin and chipotle, works so well on the seared skirt steak.

MOCHA SKIRT STEAK FAJITAS

FEEDS 4

RECOMMENDED HEAT
very high

1 kg/2¼ lb. skirt steak

3–4 tablespoons dry rub (such as CountryWoodSmoke Mocha Rub or Fajita Rub)

1 red (bell) pepper, cored, deseeded and roughly sliced

1 green (bell) pepper cored, deseeded and roughly sliced

1 orange (bell) pepper, cored, deseeded and roughly sliced

1 red onion, thinly sliced

8 tortillas

200 g/1½ cups grated Monterey Jack cheese

200 ml/1 scant cup sour cream

250 ml/1 cup guacamole

a handful of sorrel or coriander/cilantro leaves

chilli/chili sauce, to serve

Set up your wood-fired oven or barbecue for direct cooking over very high heat (around 350°C/660°F).

Sprinkle the skirt steak generously with the dry rub, then let the meat sit for 1 hour at room temperature.

Meanwhile, char the peppers and onion in a cast-iron sizzler pan in the wood-fired oven or on the barbecue.

Once the edges of the vegetables are nicely charred, place the steak on top and cook for 5–6 minutes on each side, turning and flipping to ensure the meat is seared. The steak will be medium–rare after this length of time, with an internal temperature of 55°C/130°F on a digital probe thermometer. This type of steak will toughen up if it is cooked past medium.

Slice the steak thinly across the grain and serve on tortillas with the charred vegetables, grated Monterey jack cheese, sour cream, guacamole and sorrel or coriander leaves. Serve with chilli sauce for everyone to add to their own fajitas.

GRILL TIPS

You can try adding other ingredients to the finished tortillas, such as a nice pico de gallo. This is a Mexican side dish made from freshly chopped tomatoes, onion, coriander/cilantro, salt, Serrano chilli/chile peppers and lime juice.

A solid beef sandwich is an important dish to have in your barbecue armoury. All you need is some really good bread, good beef and some hot horseradish to go alongside. When teaching my barbecue basics class, this is one of the things I like to demonstrate – a lovely barbecued topside of beef, with a hint of smoke and lots of sea salt and cracked black pepper. Best served rare and cut into thin slices.

ROTISSERIE BEEF TOPSIDE WITH CREAMY HORSERADISH

FEEDS 4–5

RECOMMENDED HEAT
moderate–high

1.5 kg/3 lb. 5 oz. rolled beef topside

sea salt and freshly ground black pepper

good-quality bread, thickly sliced, and rocket/arugula or watercress, to serve

CREAMY HORSERADISH

4 tablespoons crème fraîche

4 teaspoons creamed horseradish (or, ideally, freshly grated horseradish)

a rotisserie skewer

Set up your barbecue with a rotisserie grill for cooking over moderate–high heat (180–200°C/350–400°F) with the charcoal banked up to one side and, ideally, not directly below the beef (or the dripping fat will cause flames to flare up). Sprinkle a handful of oak chips over the coals or add a chunk of oak.

Season the beef generously with salt and black pepper – be more liberal with the seasoning than feels right. Secure the beef on the rotisserie.

Set the rotisserie going and cook the beef for 40 minutes–1 hour until the internal temperature is 52°C/125°F on a digital probe thermometer.

Remove the beef from the barbecue and let rest until the internal temperature reaches 55°C/130°F, this will take about 20–30 minutes. You can leave the beef on the rotisserie while it's resting, or remove it.

While the beef is resting, mix the crème fraîche with the horseradish in a bowl and set aside.

To serve, carve the beef and place on thick slices of bread with a handful of rocket and some of the creamy horseradish.

I'm such a lover of hanger steaks. They might not be the prettiest cut, but they are full of flavour. They can sometimes be hard to get hold of, but are worth seeking out. Here, I pair them up with some delicious king oyster mushrooms cooked in butter and a lovely 'dirty' baste, made with fresh herbs, garlic and anchovy.

HANGER STEAKS WITH DIRTY BASTE & KING OYSTER MUSHROOMS

FEEDS 2

RECOMMENDED HEAT
moderate–high

4 king oyster mushrooms

a knob/pat of butter

2 hanger steaks, about 400 g/ 14 oz. each, trimmed

Aleppo chilli flakes/hot red pepper flakes, to taste

coarse sea salt

DIRTY BASTE

2 garlic cloves

a handful of rosemary

a handful of thyme

a handful of flat-leaf parsley

150 ml/⅔ cup olive oil

1 anchovy fillet

freshly squeezed juice of ½ lemon

1 tablespoon coarse sea salt

cast-iron or heavy-duty pan

Set up your barbecue for direct cooking over moderate–high heat (180–200°C/350–400°F).

For the dirty baste, blitz up the garlic, herbs, olive oil, anchovy, lemon juice and salt in a blender until it forms a paste.

Slice the king oyster mushrooms into strips and place in the cast-iron pan with the butter. Cook over the heat until browned, then set aside.

Grill the hanger steaks over direct heat, basting the charred surface with the baste every time you turn the steaks. Cook until the internal temperature is 47°C/117°F for rare, 52°C/126°F for medium–rare or 60°C/140°F for medium on a digital probe thermometer (these steaks toughen up above this temperature, so don't go past medium).

Remove from the heat and let rest for a few minutes.

Serve the steaks with the slices of mushroom and a drizzle of the remaining baste over the top. Sprinkle over some sea salt and chilli flakes to taste.

Cooking 'dirty' does not have to be limited to small bits of steak or other quickly cooked pieces of food. As with all the techniques in this book, you can mix and match the methods. For example, if you want to slow-smoke a big chunk of beef, such as this beautiful ribeye roast joint, and then finish off with a dirty sear (that is, a reverse dirty), or sear dirty on the coals first before smoking up to medium rare, just go for it.

DIRTY RIBEYE ROAST

FEEDS 8

RECOMMENDED HEAT
low–moderate

4 kg/9 lb. ribeye roast joint

DIRTY BASTE
generous sprig of thyme

generous sprig of rosemary

generous sprig of flat-leaf parsley

2 garlic cloves

2 tablespoons sea salt

good few glugs olive oil

1 teaspoon freshly squeezed lemon juice

1 canned anchovy fillet

Remove the meat from the fridge at least a couple of hours prior to cooking and let it come to room temperature.

To make my dirty baste, blitz the fresh herbs, garlic, sea salt, olive oil, lemon juice and anchovy fillet in a food processor or using a hand blender.

Set up your barbecue with good-quality lump charcoal for two-zone (direct and indirect) cooking over low–moderate heat (around 150°C/300°F). Wait for the flames to die down before cooking.

Pop the whole joint straight onto the charcoal and cook for a few minutes on each side until it crusts up perfectly on the outside.

Place the joint on the grate indirectly away from the coals, at 150°C/300°F, and brush generously all over with the baste.

Smoke the joint indirectly with the barbecue lid down until the internal temperature reaches 46–49°C/115–120°F for rare and 55–60°C/130–140°F for medium–rare on a digital probe thermometer. Here, the roast was pulled at 46°C/115°F and left to rest until the temperature reached 47°C/116°F.

GRILL TIPS

There are so many ways to cook on a barbecue, so I suggest seeing what works best for you. A lot of barbecuing is trial and error, and mixing up wonderful, live fire-cooking techniques – in this case, smoking and dirty searing. Be bold, be confident, and have fun.

CHAPTER 2

LAMB

My family and I had a fabulous trip to Turkey a few years ago, and one of the things my kids loved to eat the most was the kofte hot off the grill. We went to one restaurant where we hired a grill and could cook as many kofte as we liked. Back at home, my lovely next-door neighbour Didem kindly shared the secrets of her own kofte recipe with me, so that I could include it in this book. And here it is for you to enjoy...

KOFTE SKEWERS

FEEDS 4

RECOMMENDED HEAT
moderate–high

250 g/9 oz. minced/ground beef

250 g/9 oz. minced/ground lamb

1 egg, lightly whisked

1 onion, grated

2 garlic cloves, grated

40 g/½ cup breadcrumbs

15 g/½ cup flat-leaf parsley, very finely chopped

1 teaspoon paprika

1 teaspoon ground cumin

1 teaspoon mild chilli/red pepper flakes

1 teaspoon freshly ground black pepper

1 teaspoon sea salt

pre-soaked wooden skewers

Place all the ingredients in a large bowl and use a pounding and folding motion with your hands to bind everything together – this takes about 5 minutes. Allow the mixture to rest for about 1 hour in the fridge.

Using your hands, form the mixture into slightly thick sausage shapes around soaked wooden skewers, then allow to rest for another hour in the fridge.

Set up your barbecue for direct cooking over moderate –high heat (180–200°C/350–400°F), with the grill grate in close proximity to the coals.

Place the kofte skewers on the grill and cook for a few minutes, turning occasionally to build up an even char all over. This will take 12–14 minutes depending on the thickness of the skewers; you're looking to get them to an internal temperature of 74°C/165°F on a digital probe thermometer.

I like to serve these kofte skewers with flatbreads, rocket, yogurt and chilli sauce.

Lamb loves fire! Simple, delicate lamb skewers cooked over fire, mouthwatering and with a subtle smoky spice mix, are hard to beat. Baharat spice mix is often overlooked, as the more floral ras el hanout spice mix is more widely used in Middle Eastern and North African dishes. The chopped fresh coriander keeps things fresh, but you could add a little chopped fresh mint or flat-leaf parsley to change things up.

BAHARAT LAMB SKEWERS

FEEDS 4

RECOMMENDED HEAT
moderate

400 g/14 oz. minced/ground lamb

3–4 teaspoons baharat spice mix

1 teaspoon sea salt

a handful of coriander/ cilantro leaves, roughly chopped

2 garlic cloves, finely chopped

1 small chilli/chile (mild–medium heat), chopped

green salad, flatbreads and chilli/chili sauce, to serve

pre-soaked wooden skewers

Set up your barbecue for direct cooking over moderate heat (around 180°C/350°F), with the grill grate in close proximity to the coals.

Mix all the ingredients together in a bowl and work with your hands until well combined.

Mould a golf ball-sized piece of the mix on to each skewer. Don't make them too big or heavy as they might fall apart.

Cook over moderate heat, moving around to cook evenly, being careful not to let the fat flare up too much and burn the kebabs/kabobs, but getting a nice caramelization on the outside. You will notice the kebabs firm up as they get to temperature. You're looking for them to get to an internal temperature of 74°C/165°F on a digital probe thermometer; they'll still be moist and juicy and perfectly cooked through.

Serve with a green salad, flatbreads and chilli sauce.

A good lamb skewer cooked over coals is pretty special, as the fat crisps up and takes on every subtle nuance of smoke and dry rub. Here, I use a wonderfully fragrant blend of Middle Eastern spices, a kind of shawarma spice mix. The shallots caramelize and add sweetness to the combination.

LAMB AND SHALLOT SKEWERS

FEEDS 4

RECOMMENDED HEAT
moderate–high

750 g/1 lb. 10 oz. lamb neck fillet, cut into 3-cm/1¼-inch cubes

6–8 shallots, halved

flatbreads, salad, yogurt, tahini, and chilli/chili sauce, to serve

SHAWARMA SPICE MIX

1 tablespoon ground coriander

1 teaspoon dried oregano

1 teaspoon ground allspice

1 teaspoon ground cinnamon

1 teaspoon ground cumin

1 teaspoon garlic powder

½ teaspoon ground ginger

½ teaspoon ground turmeric

½ teaspoon freshly ground black pepper

½ teaspoon chilli/chili powder (optional, if you like it hot)

1 teaspoon sea salt

wide, flat metal skewers

Set up your barbecue for direct cooking over moderate–high heat (180–200°C/350–400°F).

Alternately push cubes of lamb and shallot halves onto metal skewers.

Mix all the ingredients for the shawarma spice mix in a bowl, then sprinkle it over the skewers.

Start searing the skewers over direct heat on the grill, turning occasionally so the food doesn't burn – a little char is fine, though. Each skewer should take 8–10 minutes to cook; the lamb should hit an internal temperature of 60–65°C/140–150°F on a digital probe thermometer and remain slightly pink.

Enjoy the lamb skewers with some nice flatbreads, salad, yogurt, tahini and chilli sauce. Alternatively, serve with cooked rice or couscous.

Lamb cooked over fire with chimichurri is a classic taste of Argentina, and here is a simple skewer that captures these wonderful flavours. Chimichurri as a condiment is hard to beat, and lamb just loves fire. Make it the traditional way in a mortar, pounded with a pestle – it's a satisfying thing to do and you'll get the best texture and flavour out of the ingredients.

LAMB SKEWERS WITH CHIMICHURRI

FEEDS 4

RECOMMENDED HEAT
high

600 g/1 lb. 5 oz. lamb leg steaks or neck fillet, cut into 2.5-cm/1-inch cubes

3 tablespoons Aleppo chilli flakes/ hot red pepper flakes (moderate heat)

sea salt and freshly ground black pepper

1 quantity Chimichurri (see page 46)

a green salad and crusty bread, to serve

wide, flat metal skewers

Set up your barbecue for direct cooking over high heat (around 200°C/400°F).

Thread the lamb cubes onto the skewers, dust with the chilli/red pepper flakes and season with salt and freshly ground pepper.

Place the skewers onto the grill and cook until nicely charred on all sides. The internal temperature should reach 60–65°C/140–150°F on a digital probe thermometer, so the lamb stays pink and juicy.

Drizzle the chimichurri over the lamb skewers, and serve with a green salad and some crusty bread to mop up the juices.

Lamb and fire go together perfectly. Instead of the searing heat of a charcoal grill, here I wanted to recreate the gentle heat of the South American 'asado'. This plump little rack of lamb is cooked gently over the fire, but the proximity of the flames results in crisp, smoky fat too. I picked up the rack of lamb from a local meat-box delivery company, who had sourced it locally and it was excellent quality. The olive wood used for smoking here is great, giving off a gentle heat with a lovely toasty smoke.

SLOW-SMOKED LAMB RACK WITH CHIMICHURRI ROJO

FEEDS 8

RECOMMENDED HEAT
high

1.5 kg/3¼ lb. rack of lamb

4 sweet potatoes

4 large flat mushrooms

handful of spring onions/scallions

sea salt and freshly ground black pepper

CHIMICHURI ROJO

2 garlic cloves

½ red onion

a handful of flat-leaf parsley

a handful of oregano

125 ml/½ cup olive oil

1 tablespoon tomato purée/paste

a pinch of smoked paprika

a splash of red wine

sea salt

Set up your barbecue for indirect cooking over high heat (around 200°C/400°F).

To make the chimichurri rojo, blitz all the ingredients in a food processor or using a hand blender until you have a smooth-ish paste. If you wish, loosen the paste with a little more olive oil. Set aside.

Season the rack of lamb with sea salt and black pepper, to taste. Pop the rack on the barbecue next to the flame, but not directly over it. Cook gently with the lid on for about an hour. The fat will start to crisp up, but check the internal temperature of the thickest part of the meat reaches 55°C/130°F on a digital probe thermometer. Make sure to turn the rack around every 10 minutes, so the lamb cooks evenly.

While the lamb is cooking, put some sweet potatoes wrapped in foil directly on to the coals and cook, turning occasionally, until soft; this will take about 40 minutes.

Brush the chimichurri over the lamb about 5 minutes before the end of the cook, then, once cooked, remove from the heat, cover with foil, and rest for 20–30 minutes.

While the lamb rests, clean the mushrooms thoroughly, brush both sides with some chimichurri rojo, and grill over direct heat for a few minutes on each side until cooked through. Cook the spring onions directly in the embers until charred and soft.

Cut the lamb into thick, blushing cutlets and brush with some more chimichurri rojo.

Serve the lamb on a large platter with the mushrooms, spring onions and sweet potatoes.

GRILL TIPS

Grilled mushrooms are delicious with lamb. I had stumbled across a large giant puffball mushroom while out on a walk. I cut this into thick, cream-coloured slices, which I grilled over direct heat and ate with the lamb. Remember: you have to be 100 per cent sure that you have correctly identified any mushrooms you forage in the wild to avoid risk of poisoning.

This tasty little recipe is also quick and simple, which sums up the essence of good skewers – pulling something together with lots of flavour and that cooks very quickly. These are based on a hugely popular South African grill skewer called a sosatie (the name thought to come from satay). The rich cultural mixing pot of many African countries gives rise to wonderful dishes like this. The baste is curry-spiced apricot jam/preserve. I cooked these over a mix of charcoal and some embers from Camelthorn braaiwood for a nice smoky flavour.

QUICK SOSATIES

FEEDS 2

RECOMMENDED HEAT
moderate–high

500 g/1 lb. 2 oz. lamb neck fillet, cut into 3-cm/1¼-inch cubes

100 g/⅔ cup semi-soft apricots

sea salt

Grilled Veg Piri Piri Slaw (see page 131), to serve

CURRY-SPICED APRICOT BASTE

2 tablespoons apricot jam/preserve

1 garlic clove, finely chopped

1 teaspoon curry powder

1 tablespoon white wine vinegar

pre-soaked wooden skewers

Set up your barbecue for direct cooking over moderate heat (180–200°C/350–400°F), with the grill grate in close proximity to the coals.

For the baste, melt the apricot jam with the garlic, curry powder and vinegar in a small pan over the coals and stir to combine.

Alternate 2 cubes of lamb, followed by 2 apricots onto each skewer until the skewer is full, ending with a piece of lamb, not an apricot.

Season the skewers lightly with salt and place on the grill. Cook for a few minutes, then turn. You want the lamb to start to char lightly, but be careful the apricots don't burn, they just need a light char. Continue cooking, turning occasionally for about 8 minutes, then use a silicone pastry brush to cover the skewers with the apricot baste. Cook for a few more minutes, ensuring the lamb has an internal temperature of 60–65°C/140–150°F on a digital probe thermometer; about 10–12 minutes total cooking time.

Serve with grilled veg piri piri slaw, if liked.

Lamb and fire are so good together. Simply pop the meat on your skewer and dust with a spicy North African seasoning such as ras el hanout. I recall the heady fragrance of the spice markets in Marrakesh, and the flavour of this wonderful combination of lamb and ras el hanout spices hot off the grill. The charred citrus and bay leaves take this to a whole new level. Lamb neck fillet is a great cut for this – inexpensive, and tender, cooked to medium blushing pink with a charred crust.

MOROCCAN LAMB & GRILLED CITRUS SKEWERS

FEEDS 4

RECOMMENDED HEAT
moderate–high

500 g/1 lb. 2 oz. lamb neck fillet, cut into 3-cm/1¼-inch cubes

8 small citrus, such as tangerines, halved

16 fresh large bay leaves

4 tablespoons ras el hanout

sea salt and freshly ground black pepper

flatbreads, to serve

double-pronged metal skewers

Set up your barbecue for direct cooking over moderate heat (180–200°C/350–400°F), with the grill grate in close proximity to the coals.

Load up the skewers with lamb, alternating with the tangerine halves and bay leaves. Season evenly with the salt and pepper, and dust with the ras el hanout.

Place the skewers over the heat. Grill for a few minutes, then turn. Continue to cook, turning occasionally, until the lamb is crisp and charred, and has an internal temperature of 60–65°C/140–150°F on a digital probe thermometer, and the tangerines and bay leaves are slightly charred at the edges.

Serve hot, squeezing the juice from a charred tangerine over the lamb just before serving. These are great accompanied by flatbreads.

CHAPTER 3

PORK

I've been experimenting with pork scratchings – crushed up, they make a crispy coating that can be used in a similar way to breadcrumbs, while blitzing them creates a wonderful alternative to panko breadcrumbs. Here the pork 'panko' sticks perfectly to the sausagemeat skewers when you press it in and although you'll probably lose a little of it to the fire, most of it should stay attached to the sausagemeat.

CRISPY SAUSAGE BITES

FEEDS 4 (side or starter)

RECOMMENDED HEAT
low–moderate

100 g/3½ oz. pork scratchings or pork crunch

500 g/1 lb. 2 oz. good-quality pork sausagemeat

3 tablespoons barbecue dry rub seasoning of your choice

ketchup or barbecue sauce and sliced pickled jalapeños, to serve

pre-soaked wooden skewers

Set up your barbecue for direct cooking over low–moderate heat (around 140°C/280°F).

In a food processor, blitz the pork scratchings to a coarse breadcrumb consistency.

Mould golf ball-sized pieces of sausagemeat onto the skewers to make sausage shapes, sprinkle lightly with the dry rub and then coat with the pork scratching crumb, pressing it in to make it hold.

Pop onto the barbecue and cook slowly over the glowing embers for 10–12 minutes, turning occasionally, until the crumb coating is crispy and the internal temperature of the sausagemeat has reached 74°C/165°F on a digital probe thermometer.

Serve hot with a good ketchup or barbecue sauce and some slices of pickled jalalpeño.

A tasty skewer recipe with just two ingredients, how good is that? This is a wonderful taste of Spain, and is epic in its simplicity and flavour. Padrón peppers are seasonal, but because of their increasing popularity they are becoming easier to obtain (I initially struggled to get hold of them, but when I put out an emergency S.O.S. on social media, a friend told me about someone growing them less than a mile away from my home!). Although traditionally, pan-fried in olive oil until charred and sprinkled with salt flakes, they work beautifully cooked over embers too. If you can't get the padrón for whatever reason, feel free to substitute with sweet mini (bell) peppers.

CHORIZO & PADRÓN SKEWERS

FEEDS 2

RECOMMENDED HEAT
moderate

6 padrón peppers

½ horseshoe chorizo, about 200 g/7 oz. (it should be fully-cured and ready to eat, i.e. not cooking chorizo)

sea salt flakes

crusty bread, to serve

wide, flat metal skewers

Set up your barbecue for direct cooking over moderate heat (around 180°C/350°F).

Slice the chorizo into 1-cm/½-inch slices. Load up the skewers, alternating between whole peppers and slices of chorizo.

Grill for a few minutes before turning, and then turn every couple of minutes until the peppers and chorizo are slightly charred; the overall cooking time should be 7–8 minutes. As the chorizo warms up it will start to drip its oil on the coals causing flare-ups, so take care.

Serve with a sprinkle of sea salt flakes and a few chunks of crusty bread – and maybe even a glass of Spanish Rioja to wash it down.

A great way to use skewers is to thread ingredients onto them to form a raft, which can then be layered with toppings. Here I use a wonderful combination of Argentine-style chorizo sausages, melting Cheddar cheese and chimichurri. I cooked this over apple wood on a firepit my friend Richard made for me. I also made use of the thick V-bar grill to add some seared stripes to the sausages – this captured the oils and chimichurri, so I poured it over the top of my skewers when serving.

CHORIZO, CHEESE & CHIMICHURRI RAFTS

FEEDS 3

RECOMMENDED HEAT
moderate–high

6 cooking chorizo sausages

100 g/1 cup grated Cheddar cheese

crusty bread, to serve

CHIMICHURRI

2 garlic cloves

2 tablespoons Aleppo chilli flakes/ hot red pepper flakes

1 tablespoon sea salt

a handful of flat-leaf parsley, chopped

a handful of oregano leaves, chopped

2 teaspoons dried oregano

a pinch of smoked paprika

a splash of red wine vinegar

100 ml/⅓ cup extra virgin olive oil

fine metal skewers

Make the chimichurri first. In a pestle and mortar, pound the garlic, chilli flakes and salt until they form a paste, then add in the chopped fresh herbs and dried oregano and paprika, and give it a good pounding. Add the red wine vinegar and olive oil, a little at a time, and pound some more until you have a coarse paste. Cover and set aside.

Set up your barbecue for direct cooking over moderate–high heat (180–200°C/350–400°F).

Line up the chorizo sausages next to each other, and thread them onto the skewers to make a 'raft'. Place the sausage raft on the grill over the glowing embers and cook slowly for 20 minutes, turning as required until the sausages are browned all over. Use a digital probe thermometer to ensure an internal temperature of 74°C/165°F.

Sprinkle the grated cheese over the sausages while still on the grill to melt it, then top with a generous drizzle of chimichurri down the centre.

Serve with crusty bread to mop up the juices.

I love this recipe and brought the big guns out for it – my 1-metre/3-feet long churrasco skewers – and cooked the meat over apple-wood embers. It is certainly a grand skewer, but quite simple. The herb baste really makes this shine, and the Parmesan crust gives a wonderful extra savoury element that is unexpectedly good.

PORK LOIN WITH PARMESAN CRUST

FEEDS 4

RECOMMENDED HEAT
moderate–high

700 g/1 lb. 9 oz. pork loin with
5 mm–1 cm/¼–½ inch of fat on it

2 tablespoons sea salt

100 g/1⅓ cups finely grated
Parmesan cheese

HERB BASTE

a handful of rosemary, leaves
picked

a handful of thyme, leaves picked

a handful of flat-leaf parsley, leaves
picked

2 garlic cloves

50 ml/3½ tablespoons good-quality
extra virgin olive oil

freshly squeezed juice of ½ lemon

2 tablespoons sea salt

1 anchovy fillet

long, thick metal skewers

Make the herb baste first. Blitz all the ingredients in a jug/pitcher with a hand blender or in a food processor. Set aside for at least 1 hour to allow the flavours to develop.

Set up your barbecue for direct cooking over moderate–high heat (180–200°C/350–400°F).

Cut the pork loin up into 3-cm/1¼-inch cubes, then thread these onto your skewers, making sure the fat all faces the same way. Season with the salt.

Place the skewers on the grill over the glowing embers and cook for about 15 minutes, turning occasionally until the surface of the pork is brown, and give the fatty side a little extra time to help it to crisp it up. Using a silicone pastry brush, occasionally brush over the herb baste throughout cooking.

Use a digital probe thermometer to check the internal temperature of the pork and once it hits 60°C/140°F, evenly sprinkle the Parmesan cheese over the pork. Leave for a few minutes so it starts to melt, then turn the cheesy side to the heat for 1–2 minutes until the cheese forms a crust.

When you think of combinations of ingredients, you have to consider which flavours work together, as well as how quickly they cook – it's a delicate balancing act. These two make perfect companions, as sweet, sharp charred pineapple and fatty, meaty pork complement each other so well. They also cook at a similar pace, and the result is simple and very tasty.

PORK & PINEAPPLE SKEWERS

FEEDS 4

RECOMMENDED HEAT
moderate–high

500 g/1 lb. 2 oz. pork loin, with a little fat on, cut into 2.5-cm/1-inch cubes

½ pineapple, peeled and cut into 2.5-cm/1-inch cubes

sea salt

2 tablespoons runny honey

wide, flat metal skewers

Set up your barbecue for direct cooking over moderate–high heat (180–200°C/350–400°F), with the grill grate in close proximity to the coals.

Thread the pork and pineapple cubes onto skewers, alternating between the pork and pineapple. Season the pork lightly and evenly with salt.

Place the skewers over the glowing coals and grill for a few minutes on each side until the pork and pineapple are both lightly charred.

Warm the honey in a small pan, and use a silicone pastry brush to glaze the pork and pineapple lightly with it.

Cook for a few more minutes until the pork has reached an internal temperature of 63°C/145°F on a digital probe thermometer and is lightly charred.

Fatty pork belly is often paired with something sweet and sharp – usually apple sauce, which can be bland. To fix this, I've gone for pears instead. I also wanted a filling side dish to go with the pork, and opted for sweet potato wedges. The thyme and ginger beer bring all the flavours together.

PORK BELLY, PEAR & WEDGES

FEEDS 4-5

RECOMMENDED HEAT
high

1.5 kg/3 lb. 5 oz. pork belly, skin-on and boneless

4 pears, cored and quartered

4 medium sweet potatoes, cut into thick wedges

6 sprigs of thyme

330-ml/12-fl. oz. bottle of ginger beer

sea salt and freshly ground black pepper

Set up your barbecue for two-zone (direct and indirect) cooking over moderate–high heat 180–200°C/350–400°F).

Score the pork skin with a knife, pour boiling water over the skin, and dry with paper towels (this helps crackling to form). Rub a few pinches of sea salt into the skin and sprinkle a pinch on to the meat side.

Cook the pork, skin-side down, over direct heat until the skin puffs up and goes crispy; about 20 minutes. Make sure the skin doesn't burn as the fat renders.

Once you have nice crackling, move the pork to the indirect side of the barbecue and cook for a further 1½–2½ hours, with the lid down, at 180–200°C/350–400°F. The pork should be softening now and have an internal temperature of 80°C/176°F.

Put the pears and sweet potato in a cast-iron pan or skillet, scatter over the thyme and season. Pour over the ginger beer and place the pork on top. Cook with the lid on for 1 hour, ensuring it doesn't dry out – you should be left with some ginger-beer residue in the pan. When ready, the pork will reach 90–94°C/194–201°F on a probe thermometer and be soft like butter.

To serve, cut the pork belly into four large chunks, arrange the pear and sweet potato on top, and drizzle with the juices from the pan.

A good pork chop is a wonderful thing, but not easy to get right. You need the right sort of heat to ensure a good sear and crispy crackling. I love to cook pork chops over wood embers – have a searing hot side with a few flames (to which I add new wood) and a bed of embers on the other side. I used an Argentine-style firepit grill but you can use your barbecue.

COFFEE, RUM & MAPLE-GLAZED PORK CHOPS

FEEDS 2

RECOMMENDED HEAT
very high

2 pork chops, about 5 cm/2 inches thick

25 ml/1¾ tablespoons/1 shot freshly brewed espresso coffee

25 ml/1¾ tablespoons/1 shot rum

2 tablespoons maple syrup

sea salt and freshly ground black pepper

Using a high-heat-output wood (such as ash, silver birch or beech), build a fire using a Jenga method of stacking 7.5–10-cm/3–4-inch diameter splits. Light it and allow to burn down, adding new wood as needed.

Set up your firepit or barbecue for direct cooking over very high heat (around 200°C/392°F), with the grill grate about 15–20 cm/6–8 inches above the embers.

Cut the rind of the chops at 5-cm/2-inch intervals to stop the chops curling up as the crackling forms. Season with plenty of salt and black pepper.

Place a chop on the grill and hold it with tongs, skin-edge down, over the hottest part of the grill until the crackling bubbles. Repeat for the second chop, then lay both chops flat on the grill and sear both sides, moving them from the hotter to the cooler part of the grill to not burn them.

Mix together the coffee, rum and syrup to make a glaze. Cook for 15 minutes until cooked but still juicy (internal temperature of 63°C/145°F on a probe thermometer). Use a silicon brush to glaze the chops every few minutes. Allow to rest before serving.

I've always loved the Japanese way of cooking on skewers – delicate simplicity and wonderful ingredients, often with bold flavours. The shichimi togarashi spice mix has a little hit of heat and a warm spiciness, and is a blend of chilli, sesame seeds, orange zest, ginger, Sichuan pepper and seaweed – perfect for this recipe. I paired the skewers with non-Japanese but very addictive kimchi, which is a Korean side dish of salted and fermented vegetables.

TOGARASHI PORK SKEWERS

FEEDS 2

RECOMMENDED HEAT
moderate–high

200 g/7 oz. good-quality, well-marbled pork (I used Iberico)

2 teaspoons shichimi togarashi spice mix

sea salt

200 g/7 oz. kimchi, to serve (optional)

pre-soaked wooden skewers

Set up your barbecue for direct cooking over moderate– high heat (180–200°C/350–400°F), with the grill grate in close proximity to the coals.

Cut the pork into 5-mm/¼-inch thick slices and thread on to wooden skewers. Season the pork with salt and dust with the shichimi togarashi spice mix.

Grill the skewers until the pork is crispy and cooked through, a few minutes on each side, turning as required. The overall cooking time should be 6–7 minutes.

Serve the skewers on a bed of kimchi, if you like.

I'm proud of all the recipes I create, but this one is simply spectacular. I've been eating low-carb for a couple of years now, but have missed tacos. By cooking the pork shanks at a high heat, the skin turns into a wonderful crackling, and by taking the meat to 94°C/201°F, you get a juicy pulled pork, which you can then load into the crispy pork-skin 'taco shells'.

CRISPY PORK SHANK TACOS

FEEDS 2

RECOMMENDED HEAT
moderate

2 pork shanks, about
1 kg/2¼ lb. each

1 large tomato, finely chopped

2 spring onions/scallions,
finely chopped

a handful of coriander/cilantro

4 tablespoons sour cream

2 tablespoons hot sauce of your
choice, plus extra to serve

sea salt and freshly ground black
pepper

Set up your barbecue for two-zone (direct and indirect) cooking over moderate heat (160–180°C/320–350°F). Add a chunk of cherry wood to the coals for a little smoke.

Rub some salt and pepper into each pork shank and place them on the barbecue, just to the edge of the direct heat zone. Cook with the lid down until the skin crisps up to crackling; 30–40 minutes.

Once you are happy with the crackling, move the shanks to the indirect heat side to cook slowly with the lid down for 1½–2 hours until they have an internal temperature of 94°C/201°F on a probe thermometer. The meat should be tender with little resistance. Allow to rest for 20–30 minutes.

Meanwhile, mix together the chopped tomato, spring onions and most of the coriander. Season with a pinch of sea salt and black pepper.

Mix together the sour cream and hot sauce.

To serve, carefully cut the crispy pork skin into two pieces to look like taco shells. Pull the pork apart and load into the crispy pork skin taco shells. Top with the spicy cream, a little extra hot sauce and some of the fresh salsa and the remaining coriander.

Porchetta is a wonderful thing, and to my mind best cooked on a rotisserie – in fact, I think it is probably one of the best things you can cook on a rotisserie as it produces heavenly crackling. I stuffed my porchetta with some of my mate Mark's amazing 'nduja from the Duchy Charcuterie in Cornwall, England, which adds a rich, spicy fat to anything it touches.

'NDUJA-STUFFED PORCHETTA

FEEDS A CROWD

RECOMMENDED HEAT
high

2 kg/4½ lb. pork belly, skin-on and boneless

200 g/7 oz 'nduja

sea salt

a rotisserie skewer

Leave the pork belly overnight in the fridge with the skin exposed to dehydrate – this will help the crackling form.

Set up your barbecue with a rotisserie grill for cooking over high heat (around 200°C/400°F) .

Remove the pork from the fridge and spread the inside with the 'nduja. Roll up the porchetta, removing the excess skin (you don't want skin on the inside of the porchetta, or it won't crisp up).

Tie the porchetta with butcher's slip knots using heavy butcher's twine to keep it secure – you should now have a nice, barrel-shaped porchetta. (Look on YouTube to see how to tie a butcher's slip knot.)

Score the skin of the pork with a sharp knife in-between the pieces of string and rub liberally with sea salt, working this into the scores on the skin.

Slide the porchetta onto the rotisserie, using the prongs to secure it in place. Cook for a couple of hours until the skin has formed crackling, the internal temperature is at least 85°C/185°F and a skewer goes into the meat like butter.

Remove it from the spit, let rest for 15–20 minutes, then cut the porchetta into thick slices to serve.

Smoking food low and slow is great for cooking large chunks of meat until they are tender and juicy, but usually means that you won't get good crackling on a chunk of pork. There is, however, a wonderful place – between direct and indirect heat – where the meat gets to see a glancing blow of heat, but doesn't drip fat onto the coals, causing a flare-up.

ROAST PORK WITH CRISPY CRACKLING

FEEDS 4-6

RECOMMENDED HEAT
moderate

1.5–2 kg/3½–4½ lb. pork loin roasting joint, skin-on

sea salt and freshly ground black pepper

roast potatoes and green vegetables, to serve

Set up your barbecue for two-zone (direct and indirect) cooking over moderate heat (160–180°C/ 320–350°F). Add a chunk of cherry or apple wood to the coals for a gentle smoke.

Dry off the skin of the pork with some paper towels, then rub in sea salt and black pepper to taste – try to get plenty into the scores of the skin.

Place the pork on the barbecue with the skin side facing the lit charcoal – 10–15 cm/4–6 inches from the edge of the coals. Put the lid on the barbecue, but keep an eye on the skin to ensure it doesn't burn. The skin should start puffing up to form crackling. If it doesn't, move the joint slightly closer to the charcoal, but be wary of burning the crackling.

Once you have the crackling as you like it, move the pork away from the coals – about 20 cm/8 inches is ideal – and cook with the lid on for 30–40 minutes until the internal temperature reaches 63°C/145°F for medium and 71°C/160°F for well done. Remove from the barbecue and let rest for 20–30 minutes.

Cut the pork into thick slices and serve with the roast potatoes and your choice of green vegetables.

CHAPTER 4

POULTRY & GAME

A chicken lollipop is a wondrous thing: a juicy, bite-size nugget of chicken-drumstick meat with its own built-in 'handle'. Here, I layer the drumsticks with some great flavour combinations that seem a bit out of the ordinary, but work well – give it a try!

CHILLI MARMALADE GLAZED CHICKEN LOLLIPOPS

FEEDS 1-2

RECOMMENDED HEAT
moderate

4 chicken drumsticks

2 tablespoons CountryWoodSmoke Mocha Rub (or your favourite barbecue dry rub)

GLAZE

2 tablespoons sweet chilli sauce (such as Linghams)

2 tablespoons fine-cut orange marmalade

Set up your barbecue for two-zone (direct and indirect) cooking over moderate heat (160–180°C/320–350°F). Adding a chunk of hickory wood to the coals gives a nice smoke, but cherry and apple wood are good, too.

To prepare the chicken lollipops, cut through the tendons and gently pull back the skin and muscle of each drumstick to expose the bone and create a lollipop handle. Dust the lollipops lightly and evenly with the dry rub.

Pop the lollipops on the barbecue and cook with the lid on. Turn/move the lollipops, as required between direct and indirect heat, so they cook evenly and the skin crisps up. The lollipops should take about 30 minutes to reach an internal temperature of 60°C/140°F on a digital probe thermometer.

In a small bowl, mix together the chilli sauce and marmalade to make the glaze. Brush the glaze evenly over the lollipops with a pastry or silicone brush, then cook for a further 10 minutes, ensuring the chicken reaches an internal temperature of 74°C/165°F throughout. Serve and enjoy!

I was set a challenge at a demo by a chef friend of mine, to come up with a new idea for grilled chicken thighs and this was the outcome. The sauce is my CountryWoodSmoke twist on an Alabama white sauce (see page 78), relatively unknown in the UK, which is a shame as it goes so well with chicken and turkey.

GRILLED CHICKEN THIGHS WITH PICKLED WHITE BARBECUE SAUCE

FEEDS 1

RECOMMENDED HEAT
moderate

2 boneless chicken thighs, skin-on

2 teaspoons barbecue dry rub (such as CountryWoodSmoke House Rub)

selection of pickles, to serve

PICKLED WHITE BARBECUE SAUCE

6 tablespoons good-quality mayonnaise

2 tablespoons cider vinegar

3 pickled gherkins, finely diced

1 tablespoon pickle juice (from the jar of pickled gherkins)

1 tablespoon American yellow mustard

1 teaspoon white sugar

1 garlic clove, mashed to a pulp

1 teaspoon creamed horseradish

2 teaspoons freshly ground black pepper

sea salt

Set up your barbecue for direct cooking over moderate heat (160–180°C/320–350°F). Add a chunk of hickory wood to the coals to smoke.

Make the sauce in advance by mixing all the ingredients together in a bowl.

Remove the bones from the chicken thighs, if necessary. Boneless chicken thighs are flatter and therefore cook more evenly, while the skin also crisps up better.

Sprinkle the dry rub lightly and evenly over the thighs, on both the skin and meat side.

Cook the thighs, skin-side down, on the grill for 10–15 minutes to render the fat and crisp up the skin. Turn the thighs over and cook for a further 5 minutes, ensuring the internal temperature has reached 74°C/165°F on a digital probe thermometer.

Serve the chicken thighs with a drizzle of the barbecue sauce and a few pickles on the side. (Cover any unused sauce and store in the fridge; it should keep for a week.)

You've got to love a rotisserie chicken – juicy and delicious with beautifully crisp skin and spinning it over hot coals ensures it cooks evenly. This is a popular recipe that many people enjoy in Australia, and not surprisingly as it's full-flavoured and very easy to do. If you don't have a rotisserie, by all means just cook it in a regular kettle barbecue with a lid.

LEMON, THYME & GARLIC ROTISSERIE CHICKEN

FEEDS 4

RECOMMENDED HEAT
moderate–high

1 medium chicken (1.3–1.5 kg/ 3–3¼ lb.)

2 garlic cloves, finely chopped

leaves from 8 sprigs of fresh thyme

2 tablespoons olive oil

1 lemon, quartered

sea salt and freshly ground black pepper

a rotisserie skewer

Set up your barbecue with a rotisserie grill for cooking over moderate–high heat (180–200°C/ 350–400°F), with a distance of 20–30 cm/8–12 inches from the coals to the chicken and with the lid of the barbecue on (not essential, but it will take longer without the lid).

Place the chicken on the rotisserie skewer and secure firmly.

Place the garlic, thyme and olive oil in a small bowl and squeeze in the juice from one of the lemon quarters. Stir together, then brush this mixture all over the chicken. Season the outside generously with salt and pepper, and place the remaining lemon quarters inside the chicken.

Cook the chicken for about 1 hour until it has an internal temperature of 74°C/165°F on a digital probe thermometer.

Cut the chicken into quarters and serve with a green salad on the side, if liked.

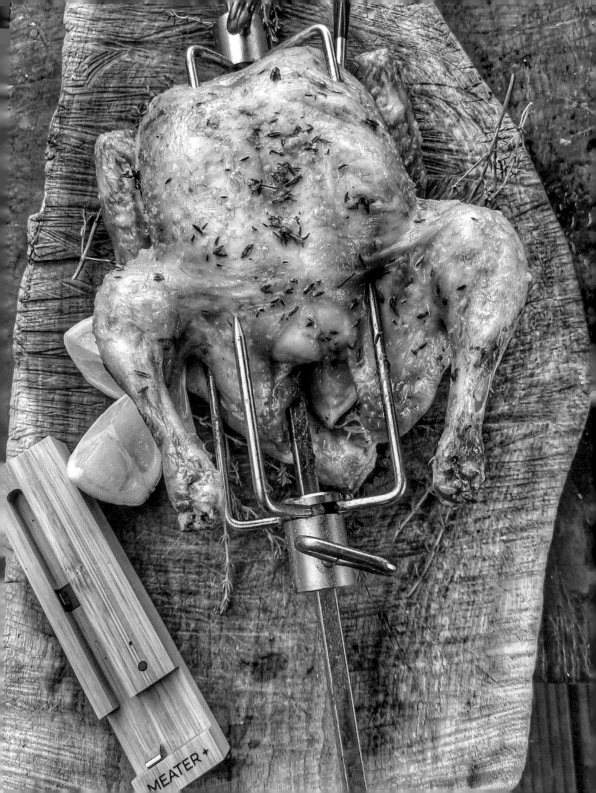

Chicken marinated in spiced yogurt, crispy at the edges but still juicy on the inside, is so good. The ideal would be to cook this in a tandoor oven, but as this is something most of us don't have at home, grilling over high heat coals does an admirable job, achieving a charred crust without drying the chicken out. Subtly spiced chicken thighs work perfectly here and stay nicely juicy.

TANDOOR-STYLE CHICKEN SKEWERS

FEEDS 4

RECOMMENDED HEAT
high

6 tablespoons natural/plain yogurt, plus extra to serve

3 tablespoons tandoori masala spice blend

freshly squeezed juice of ½ lime

2 tablespoons finely chopped coriander/cilantro, plus extra to serve

a pinch of chilli/hot red pepper flakes

500 g/1 lb. 2 oz. skinless, boneless chicken thighs

sea salt and freshly ground black pepper

double-pronged metal skewers

In a bowl mix the yogurt, tandoori masala spice blend, lime juice, coriander, chilli flakes, salt and freshly ground black pepper. Stir until combined.

Slice the chicken thighs into 4-cm/1½-inch strips and place into the yogurt marinade. Stir gently until the chicken is coated in the marinade, then leave for a couple of hours in the fridge.

Set up your barbecue for direct cooking over high heat (around 200°C/400°F), with the coals close to the grill grates for close proximity grilling.

Thread the chicken thighs onto the skewers. Place the skewers on the grill for a few minutes on each side until starting to char, turning occasionally. Total cooking time should be around 12 minutes; ensure the chicken has reached an internal temperature of 74°C/165°F on a digital probe thermometer.

Serve with a drizzle of yogurt and sprinkle with extra chopped coriander.

I love buffalo wings. Hot, vinegary, buttery, crispy and delicious – you can't just have a couple, you've got to keep digging in. To save constantly flipping and turning each individual wing, I thought they would work really well cooked on skewers to give them a nice even heat to create a crispy skin.

BUFFALO WING SKEWERS

FEEDS 4

RECOMMENDED HEAT
moderate–high

1.5 kg/3¼ lb. chicken wings, drums and flats, separated out to cook individually

4 tablespoons barbecue dry rub for poultry of your choice

30 g/2 tablespoons butter

70 ml/5 tablespoons hot sauce (the original is Frank's)

both flat and double-pronged metal skewers

Set up your barbecue for direct cooking over moderate–high heat (180–200°C/350–400°F).

Load the chicken wings up onto metal skewers. Use flat skewers for the drums and double-pronged skewers for the flats – this way they hold the chicken better.

Dust the chicken with the dry rub and place the skewers over the hot coals to cook for about 10 minutes, turning occasionally to build up a char all over them.

To make the buffalo sauce, add the butter and hot sauce to a metal pan and set it directly on the coals. Stir until the butter has melted and it's all combined.

Once the wings are crispy and slightly charred, use a digital probe thermometer to check you have a minimum internal temperature of 74°C/165°F. Take them off the heat, arrange the wings on a serving platter and pour the warm buffalo sauce over the top.

Get stuck in and eat with your fingers.

Many people are surprised that you can grill avocados, but it definitely works well – the edges char up and the flesh takes on a good flavour from any charcoal smoke. Wrap the chunks of avocado in crispy bacon, and you're on to a winner. You can glaze with whatever works for you, but this honey and sriracha chilli sauce glaze is a treat.

GLAZED CHICKEN, BACON & AVOCADO SKEWERS

FEEDS 2

RECOMMENDED HEAT
high

10 slices of streaky/fatty bacon

1 large ripe (but not overly ripe) avocado, cut into 3-cm/1¼-inch pieces

2 skinless chicken breasts, cut into 3-cm/1¼-inch cubes

sea salt and freshly ground black pepper

warm wraps or submarine rolls, to serve

GLAZE

2 tablespoons runny honey

2 teaspoons sriracha chilli/chili sauce, plus extra to serve

pre-soaked flat wooden skewers

Set up your barbecue with red-hot lump charcoal for direct cooking over high heat (around 200°C/400°C).

Mix together the honey and chilli sauce for the glaze, then set aside.

Cut the slices of bacon in half and wrap around the avocado pieces.

Alternately thread the cubes of chicken and bacon-wrapped avocado pieces onto the skewers. Season lightly – a pinch of sea salt and black pepper on each skewer should suffice.

Grill the skewers on the red-hot grill, turning as necessary. Ensure the chicken reaches an internal temperature of 74°C/165°F on a digital probe thermometer; it should take 8–10 minutes to cook and be slightly crispy at the edges.

Brush the skewers evenly with the glaze, before grilling for the last couple of minutes.

Serve the skewers in warm wraps or submarine rolls with some extra sriracha chilli sauce.

The chicken on these simple skewers is a juicy blank canvas for the chimichurri rojo, which really lifts the flavour here. Often you can keep things simple with skewers and just take them to the next level with the sauce, marinade or baste you use.

CHICKEN & RAMIRO PEPPER SKEWERS WITH CHIMICHURRI ROJO

FEEDS 4

RECOMMENDED HEAT
moderate

500 g/1 lb. 2 oz. skinless, boneless chicken thighs, cut into 2.5-cm/ 1-inch wide slices

2 ramiro red peppers, sliced into strips

sea salt and freshly ground black pepper

CHIMICHURRI ROJO

2 garlic cloves

½ red onion, diced

a handful of flat-leaf parsley

a handful of oregano

50 ml/⅓ cup extra virgin olive oil

1 teaspoon smoked paprika

1 teaspoon dried oregano

1 tablespoon red wine vinegar

1 tablespoon tomato pureé/paste

sea salt

pre-soaked short wooden skewers

You can either make a coarse chimichurri rojo in a pestle and mortar (see method for chimichurri on page 46), or a finer paste by blitzing the ingredients in a mini chopper. Either way, pound or blitz until you have a paste and loosen it up if necessary with a little extra olive oil. Cover and set aside to let the flavours develop for at least 30 minutes.

Set up your barbecue for direct cooking over moderate heat (around 180°C/350°F), with the coals close to the grill grates for close proximity grilling.

On soaked wooden skewers alternately thread a piece of chicken thigh and a slice of pepper until everything is used up.

Season the skewers with salt and freshly ground pepper and place on the grill. Cook for a few minutes, then turn and cook for a few more. Continue cooking, turning occasionally for an overall cooking time of 12–14 minutes. The chicken and pepper should be slightly charred and the chicken should have reached an internal temperature of 74°C/165°F on a digital probe thermometer.

Serve the skewers with the chimichurri rojo drizzled over the top.

I love a good piña colada cocktail in the summer, and this quick recipe definitely has summer written all over it. A tasty combination of coconut milk, pineapple and rum, charred to perfection alongside juicy caramelized chunks of fresh pineapple on the same skewer.

PIÑA COLADA CHICKEN SKEWERS

FEEDS 4

RECOMMENDED HEAT
moderate

400 g/14 oz. skinless chicken breasts, cut into 3-cm/1¼-inch cubes

½ pineapple, peeled and cut into 3-cm/1¼-inch cubes

coarse sea salt and black pepper

flatbreads, toasted shredded coconut (optional) and your favourite hot sauce, to serve

PIÑA COLADA MARINADE

50 ml/3½ tablespoons creamy canned coconut milk

80 g/3 oz. pineapple, chopped

25 ml/1 oz. rum

a pinch of sea salt

flat metal skewers

Make the Piña Colada marinade by blending all the ingredients together in a food processor to achieve a smooth liquid.

Place the chicken cubes in a large bowl. Pour the marinade over the chicken and stir until the cubes are fully coated. Cover the bowl and place in the fridge for 1 hour to marinate, during which time the coating should thicken up.

Set up your barbecue for direct cooking over moderate heat (around 180°C/350°F), with the coals close to the grill grates for close proximity grilling.

Load the marinated chicken breast cubes onto your skewers, alternating with the pineapple chunks. Season lightly with salt and freshly ground black pepper.

Cook over the coals until both the chicken and pineapple are lightly charred and the chicken is cooked through (it has reached an internal temperature of 74°C/165°F on a digital probe thermometer).

Enjoy the chicken loaded up into the wraps with a sprinkle of toasted coconut (if you like) and a splash of hot sauce.

Dukkah is a wonderfully crunchy Egyptian/Middle Eastern topping that works so well with this sweet honey and cumin-glazed chicken, adding a lovely textural contrast and a hint of spice. Dukkah makes a great accompaniment to a few of the skewer recipes in this chapter so make a batch and store it in a screw-top jar.

PISTACHIO DUKKAH & HONEY CHICKEN SKEWERS

FEEDS 4

RECOMMENDED HEAT
moderate–high

500 g/1 lb. 2 oz. skinless chicken breasts, cut into 3-cm/1¼-inch cubes

2 tablespoons honey

2 teaspoons cumin seeds

sea salt

PISTACHIO DUKKAH

4 tablespoons shelled pistachios

2 teaspoons sesame seeds

1 teaspoon ground coriander

1 teaspoon ground cumin

½ teaspoon fine sea salt

½ teaspoon coarsely ground black pepper

flat metal skewers

Set up your barbecue for direct cooking over moderate–high heat (180–200°C/350–400°F).

In a small pan/skillet over the coals, toast the dukkah ingredients lightly for a few minutes, then smash up in a pestle and mortar or blitz briefly in a food processor, but don't make them too fine. Set aside.

Load the chicken cubes onto your skewers and season lightly with salt.

Grill the chicken over the coals for a few minutes on each side until just starting to char slightly. Place the honey and cumin seeds in a small pan to warm through slightly (keep an eye on it as the honey will quickly caramelize and burn if you aren't careful) and brush onto the chicken using a pastry or silicone brush. The chicken is ready when caramelized and has reached an internal temperature of 74°C/165°F on a digital probe thermometer.

Sprinkle generously with the pistachio dukkah and enjoy hot.

I've always admired the simple elegance of Japanese cooking, especially the skewers. A chicken yakitori is a great recipe to have up your sleeve, using chicken thighs, spring onions and a delicious glaze called 'tare' (teriyaki is a version of this).

CHICKEN YAKITORI

FEEDS 2

RECOMMENDED HEAT
moderate

500 g/1 lb. 2 oz. boneless chicken thighs, skin removed and reserved

4 spring onions/scallions

sea salt

TARE SAUCE

250 ml/1 cup dark soy sauce

250 ml/1 cup sake

125 ml/½ cup mirin

125 g/⅔ cup sugar

25 g/1 oz. ginger root, unpeeled

pre-soaked wooden skewers

Put the sauce ingredients in a pan and simmer slowly, stirring occasionally, for 1 hour until reduced by half.

Set up your barbecue for close proximity grilling over moderate heat (around 180°C/350°F) with no flame; aim to have a hotter part and a gentler heat part.

Set aside 4 large thigh pieces and cut the rest of the meat into 1-cm/½-inch pieces. Thread onto skewers.

Cut 2 of the skin sections in half, then wrap around the larger thigh pieces. Thread a skewer through, making sure you secure the skin, then add a piece of spring onion, another skin-wrapped thigh piece and another piece of spring onion. Repeat for a second skewer. Thread any leftover chicken skin pieces onto the skewers too. You should have 2 chicken-and-spring onion skewers, 6–8 thigh-meat yakitori, and a few chicken-skin skewers. Season lightly with salt.

Cook the chicken-and-spring onion skewers for a few minutes on each side on the hot part of the grill to crisp the skin. Then move them to the moderate heat to cook through, brushing with the tare sauce. Cook the chicken-skin skewers over the moderate part of the grill for 10–12 minutes to crisp up. Cook the thigh skewers over the hotter section, turning every couple of minute, and brushing with the sauce.

Check all the chicken has reached 74°C/165°F using a digital probe thermometer.

Duck is great cooked on the grill, especially when the skin and fat become crispy. It's perfect for skewer cooking as you can cut slices of the duck, pop them on the skewer and then add a delicious glaze, such as this honey and sriracha combination, which has a lovely balance of sweet and heat, and has to be one of my favourite sauces.

HONEY & SRIRACHA-GLAZED DUCK SKEWERS

FEEDS 2

RECOMMENDED HEAT
moderate–high

1 duck breast, sliced across its width into 1-cm/½-inch slices

1 tablespoon runny honey

1 tablespoon sriracha hot sauce

a few sprigs of rosemary, to garnish (optional)

sea salt and freshly ground black pepper

rice, to serve (optional)

pre-soaked small bamboo/ wooden skewers

Set up your barbecue for direct cooking over moderate–high heat (180–200°C/350–400°F), with the coals close to the grill grates for close proximity grilling.

Thread the duck through the widest parts onto the skewers, ensuring you pierce the skin at both ends to secure. Season once all the duck is on the skewers.

Stir the honey and Sriracha together in a small bowl.

Grill the duck skewers for a few minutes on each side until brown, then use a pastry or silicone brush to brush on the spicy sweet glaze. Grill for 1–2 minutes per side until the glaze is seared in. Make sure the internal temperature has reached 74°C/165°F on a digital probe thermometer.

Enjoy with a side of rice if you like, and a cold beer.

All too often with duck, it's the breast that gets most attention when it comes to cooking, but the leg meat is dark, juicy and delicious. It needs a lot more cooking than the breast, otherwise it remains tough, but if you get the temperature just right, it will be amazing. It works perfectly with a touch of cherry or beech smoke, and a sweet glaze. Adding smoke to roasting meat makes it even more tasty with the additional benefit of crispy skin.

SMOKY SWEET DUCK LEGS

FEEDS 2

RECOMMENDED HEAT
moderate

2 duck legs

2 tablespoons runny honey

1 teaspoon Aleppo chilli flakes/hot red pepper flakes

sea salt and freshly ground black pepper

salad leaves, to serve

Set up your barbecue for direct cooking at a moderate heat (160–180°C/320–350°F). Add a chunk of beech or cherry wood for smoke.

Using a sharp knife, pierce the skin all over the duck legs to help the fat render and the skin to crisp up. Season the duck legs with sea salt and black pepper.

Cook the duck legs just to the edge of the direct heat, skin-side down, over a tray to catch the duck fat (perfect for cooking roast potatoes or the Duck Fat Garlic Scallops on page 86). Cook with the lid on for around 40 minutes until the duck reaches an internal temperature of about 85°C/185°F, at which point some of the collagen will have broken down to make the meat tender.

Mix together the honey and chilli flakes and brush this mixture onto the smoked duck legs. Smoke the legs with the lid down for 5–10 minutes for the glaze to set, then serve with salad leaves.

For many people, turkey is served only once a year, but I'm a big fan of this meat at any time. Away from the festive season, it provides tasty, good-quality meat, which, if cooked well with a lick of smoke, bears no resemblance to the cardboard turkey of many festive meals. Turkey thighs are even better value for money than the white meat. I love them – they pull so well, and should be on everyone's smoker. I went for some lovely cherry smoke to give the meat a nice pink smoke ring and a sweet smoked taste. A smoke ring is a slightly pink ring that forms on the edge of smoked meats in a complex interaction of the meat and smoke/combustion gases. The Alabama white sauce is awesome, especially on smoked turkey and chicken.

PULLED TURKEY WITH ALABAMA WHITE SAUCE

FEEDS 4

RECOMMENDED HEAT
low–moderate

750 g–1 kg/1 lb. 10 oz.–2¼ lb. turkey thighs, bone-in and skin-on (you don't need to be exact with weight, because you are cooking to temperature rather than time)

barbecue dry rub of your choice (one that goes well with pulled pork is ideal)

brioche rolls, Simple Coleslaw (see page 130) and pickled gherkins, to serve

ALABAMA WHITE SAUCE

6 tablespoons good-quality mayonnaise

3 tablespoons cider vinegar

1 tablespoon American yellow mustard

1 teaspoon white sugar

1 garlic clove, mashed to a pulp

1 teaspoon creamed horseradish

sea salt and freshly ground black pepper

Set up your barbecue for indirect cooking over low–moderate heat (around 140°C/280°F), adding some chunks of cherry wood to the coals to give a nice smoke.

Dust the turkey thighs with the dry rub.

Smoke the turkey indirectly on the barbecue with the lid on for around 4–5 hours until the internal temperature of the meat reaches 80°C/176°F on a digital probe thermometer. There's no need to take the temperature as high as you do for pulled pork, as turkey doesn't have the same collagen to break down to allow it to be pulled apart.

While the thighs are smoking, mix together the Alabama white sauce ingredients, and set aside.

Once the turkey is cooked, use two forks to pull the meat apart.

Slice each brioche roll in half, toast lightly on the barbecue, and then load up with the coleslaw and pulled turkey. Drizzle with the Alabama white sauce and finish with a pickled gherkin each.

So many people dismiss turkey as a dry and unexciting meat, but if cooked to the correct internal temperature it stays juicy. Baste it with a spicy butter and it's far from bland. I was hugely inspired by my good friend Nila Ross-Patel who runs Indian barbecue classes at UK BBQ School – she cooked the most amazing butter-stuffed turkey breast as part of her practice run for a Christmas class. This is a simplified, yet still delicious, version of her recipe.

BUTTER-SPICED TURKEY

FEEDS 4-6

RECOMMENDED HEAT
moderate

1 turkey breast, about
1.5–2 kg/3¼–4½ lb.

100 g/7 tablespoons salted butter

2 teaspoons masala spice mix
(I used a korma spice mix as my
kids like it mild)

2 teaspoons ground turmeric

sea salt and freshly ground black
pepper

a handful of coriander/cilantro,
to garnish (optional)

Set up your barbecue for indirect cooking at a moderate heat (around 180°C/350°F).

Place the turkey breast, skin-side up, on a baking sheet that will fit in your barbecue with the lid on.

Melt the butter and stir in the spice mix and turmeric. Brush the spiced butter onto the turkey breast using a pastry or silicone brush and season with salt and pepper.

Place the baking sheet with the turkey in the barbecue and cook over indirect heat for around 40 minutes with the lid on, brushing occasionally with the spiced butter. The internal temperature should reach 74°C/165°F on a digital probe thermometer. Remove from the barbecue and let it rest for a good 20 minutes.

Slice the turkey breast and serve garnished with coriander, if liked.

CHAPTER 5

FISH & SEAFOOD

I love large prawns with a charred shell cooked over a high heat, but a little fatty, spicy, melted 'nduja (spicy, spreadable pork sausage) butter and a squeeze of fresh lime juice makes them particularly delicious.

PRAWNS WITH 'NDUJA & LIME

FEEDS 2

RECOMMENDED HEAT
high

240 g/8½ oz. large shell-on prawns/jumbo shrimp or wild red shrimp

1 tablespoon light olive oil

30 g/2 tablespoons butter

2 tablespoons 'nduja

freshly squeezed juice of 1 lime

1 tablespoon chopped flat-leaf parsley

sea salt and freshly ground black pepper

crusty bread, to serve

small cast-iron or heavy-duty pan

Set up your barbecue for direct cooking over high heat (around 200°C/400°F).

Toss the prawns in the oil and season lightly.

Place the prawns on the grill and cook for a few minutes, then turn and continue to cook until they are pink, cooked through and the shells charred. Set aside.

Melt the butter and 'nduja together in the cast-iron pan over the barbecue. Add the prawns and stir to coat, then squeeze over the lime juice and sprinkle over the chopped flat-leaf parsley.

Serve with crusty bread to mop up the pan juices.

It's traditional to cook scallops in a garlic, lemon and herb butter, but cooking them in duck fat is a lovely alternative. You can get duck fat hotter than butter without it burning, thus improving the sear and caramelization on the scallops. I love my scallops with the creamy sweet orange roe left attached.

DUCK FAT GARLIC SCALLOPS

FEEDS 2

RECOMMENDED HEAT
moderate

1 tablespoon duck fat

12 scallops with roe

freshly squeezed juice of
½ lemon

1 garlic clove, finely chopped

1 tablespoon chopped
flat-leaf parsley

sea salt and freshly ground
black pepper

cast-iron or heavy-duty pan

Set up your barbecue for direct cooking over moderate heat (160–180°C/320–350°F).

Place your pan directly on the coals or close to them on the grill grate. Allow the pan to warm up a few minutes.

Add the duck fat to the hot pan. After 20–30 seconds, when the fat is sizzling, add the scallops. Cook for 2–3 minutes until seared and caramelized, then turn to sear and caramelize the other side.

Add the lemon juice and garlic for the final minute of cooking, then, once cooked, add the parsley and season with a pinch of salt and pepper.

Serve at once.

Scallops are plump and sweet, but a glaze of light maple syrup and some fruity chilli flakes really complement their flavour. The beetroot have a delicious earthy sweetness and the kale, when crisp, resembles seaweed.

MAPLE & CHILLI SCALLOPS WITH BEETROOT AND KALE

FEEDS 2

RECOMMENDED HEAT
moderate

2 small beetroot/beets

8 scallops with roe

4 teaspoons maple syrup

1 teaspoon Aleppo chilli flakes/hot red pepper flakes

a handful of kale

1 teaspoon extra virgin olive oil, plus extra to drizzle

sea salt

lemon wedges, to serve

2 flat metal skewers

Set up your barbecue for direct cooking over moderate heat (around 180°C/350°F).

Place the beetroot directly into the embers and cook for 20–30 minutes until the outside is charred and the inside softened, then set aside until cool enough to handle.

Thread four scallops onto each skewer and season with salt.

Cook the scallops over direct heat for 3–4 minutes on each side until lightly brown.

Lightly brush the scallops with the maple syrup using a pastry or silicon brush and dust with the chilli flakes, then cook for a minute more on each side, ensuring the internal temperature doesn't go higher than 55°C/131°F on a digital probe thermometer.

Toss the kale in the olive oil and place directly over the coals to crisp up (you can use a metal sieve/strainer placed onto the coals for this).

Thinly slice the beetroot, then plate up with the crispy kale and scallops. Season with a pinch of sea salt and drizzle with a little olive oil. Serve with lemon wedges for squeezing over.

Langoustines are a real treat. Here they are cooked simply on a hot grill and smothered in a garlic, herb and lemon butter. They are sweet and delicious.

GRILLED GARLIC BUTTER LANGOUSTINES

FEEDS 2

RECOMMENDED HEAT
moderate–high

20 langoustines

50 g/3½ tablespoons butter

1 garlic clove, finely chopped

freshly squeezed juice of
½ lemon

2 tablespoons chopped
flat-leaf parsley

sea salt and freshly ground
black pepper

lemon wedges, to serve

small cast-iron or heavy-duty
pan

Set up your barbecue for direct cooking over moderate–high heat (180–200°C/350–400°F).

Place the langoustines on the grill and cook over direct heat for 5–6 minutes, turning occasionally, until they have an internal temperature of 55–60°C/131–140°F on a digital probe thermometer. Season with salt and pepper and set aside.

Melt the butter in the pan and add the garlic, lemon juice and parsley.

Arrange the langoustines on a platter or two plates and pour over the melted garlic, herb and lemon butter.

Serve at once with lemon wedges.

Having some sort of heavy-duty pot with a lid to cook on a barbecue is a real bonus and opens up so many wonderful cooking opportunities. Some simply cooked mussels over a fire are one of my favourite things to eat, served in a big bowl with a chunk or two of crusty bread to dip in the juices.

MUSSELS IN BEER

FEEDS 2

RECOMMENDED HEAT
moderate

15 g/1 tablespoon butter

2 garlic cloves, finely chopped

1 kg/2¼ lb. live mussels, debearded

200 ml/scant 1 cup light beer, such as lager or fruity IPA

freshly squeezed juice of ½ lemon

2 tablespoons chopped flat-leaf parsley

sea salt and freshly ground black pepper

chunks of rustic bread, such as focaccia or sourdough, to serve

cast-iron Dutch oven or heavy-duty pan with a lid

Set up your barbecue for direct cooking over moderate heat (around 160°C/320°F). You can also use a firepit or wood-fired oven.

Put the cast-iron Dutch oven or pan on the barbecue to get hot, either straight in the coals or on a grill grate just over the coals.

Melt the butter in the hot pan, then add the garlic, followed by the mussels. Cook for a minute, then add the beer. Pop the lid on the pan and allow to steam for 5–6 minutes until the mussels are open and cooked through. Discard any mussels that remain closed.

Season lightly to taste, squeeze over the lemon juice and sprinkle the chopped parsley over the top. Serve at once with some bread for mopping up the juices.

Simple grilled prawns on skewers with a squeeze of lemon are wonderful, but here I wanted to go down a slightly different route, and give them a glaze of honey and a bit of bite with a sweet, slightly crunchy toasted coconut coating. I found it quite hard to keep all of the coconut on the prawns, and lost a bit of it as a sacrifice to the coals... but there was enough that stayed in place to give these a lovely texture and taste.

COCONUT HONEY PRAWN SKEWERS

FEEDS 2

RECOMMENDED HEAT
moderate–high

12 king prawns/jumbo shrimp

2 tablespoons runny honey

4 tablespoons toasted coconut flakes, blitzed in a food processor

sea salt

coriander/cilantro and lime wedges, to serve

pre-soaked small wooden skewers

Set up your barbecue for close proximity cooking over moderate–high heat (180–200°C/350–400°F).

If your prawns are shell on, remove the shell in the mid section, keeping the head and tail on for presentation. Also remove the dark line of the intestine.

Thread three prawns on each wooden skewer, making sure to skewer the tail end and head end to make them secure. Season with a pinch of salt, then drizzle the honey over the prawns to make them nice and sticky. Sprinkle over the toasted coconut so the prawns are evenly coated.

Place the skewers onto the hot grill and cook, turning every couple of minutes until the prawns are pink, slightly charred and have reached an internal temperature of 55°C/130°F on a digital probe thermometer.

Serve with some coriander and lime wedges for squeezing over the top.

When I was growing up we used little pots of Dunn's River Mild Curry Powder for all sorts of curries – spices back then tended to be a bit less regional and more generic, so this mild Caribbean curry mix would be used for basically any style of curry we ate. It's a great spice, subtle and fruity, and often disregarded in favour of its hotter jerk neighbour. But try it in a coconut-based marinade for these cubes of monkfish and you'll be surprised.

COCONUT CURRY MONKFISH

FEEDS 2

RECOMMENDED HEAT
very high

1 large monkfish tail fillet
(about 400 g/14 oz.), cut into
2.5-cm/1-inch cubes

coriander/cilantro and lime
wedges, to serve

MARINADE

6 tablespoons coconut milk

2 teaspoons Dunn's River
Mild Caribbean Curry
Powder

freshly squeezed juice of
½ a lime

1 teaspoon finely chopped
Scotch bonnet chilli/chile
(optional)

sea salt and freshly ground
black pepper

very thin metal skewers or
double-pronged skewers

Make the marinade by mixing all the ingredients together in a large shallow bowl.

Add the monkfish cubes to the marinade in the bowl, cover and allow to marinate in the fridge for 2 hours.

Set up your barbecue for close proximity cooking over searing hot coals (around 200°C/392°F).

Remove the monkfish cubes from the marinade and thread them onto your skewers.

Place the skewers on the grill close to the red hot coals and cook for a few minutes, then turn. Cook until seared on the outside and the fish is cooked through. Use a digital probe thermometer to ensure an internal temperature of 55°C/130°F so that the monkfish is fully cooked, but not drying out.

Serve with fresh coriander and lime wedges for squeezing over the top.

Many years ago I travelled to Kerala in southern India and have fond memories of dining in a cliff-top restaurant where you could select seafood – choosing between tuna, swordfish and prawns as big as your forearm – which were loaded onto large skewers, brushed with a spice mix and then popped into a tandoor to crisp up, the quick cooking making sure the fish stayed moist. Fresh naan breads were cooked on the walls of the tandoor too – I remember the smells and tastes of the freshly cooked food were wonderful and the seafood loaded onto the hot naan tasted heavenly. And so here I have tried to recreate some of that magic for you on the barbecue.

TANDOOR SEAFOOD SKEWERS

FEEDS 2

RECOMMENDED HEAT
very high

3 tablespoons coconut oil

2 teaspoons tandoori masala spice mix

freshly squeezed juice of ½ lime, plus ½ to squeeze on at the end

a selection of seafood, ideally nothing too delicate – I used a thick hake fillet, chunky tuna steak and some large shell-on king prawns/jumbo shrimp

sea salt

coconut rice and naan bread, to serve

thin or flat long metal skewers

Set up your barbecue for close proximity cooking over searing hot coals (around 200°C/392°F).

Melt the coconut oil in a small bowl and stir in the spice mix and lime juice.

Cut the larger fillets of fish into 3–4-cm/1¼–1½-inch cubes and thread onto skewers, alternating the pieces of fish and prawns.

Brush the loaded skewers evenly with the spiced coconut oil. Season lightly with sea salt.

Place the skewers over the coals – the heat should be blisteringly hot, but without too many flames.

Cook for a few minutes until lightly charred, then turn and cook for a few minutes more until cooked through; the cooking time will be 6–7 minutes and the internal temperature should be 55°C/130°F on a digital probe thermometer.

Squeeze over the juice from the extra lime half and serve with coconut rice and naan bread.

A fabulous technique for ensuring that you don't have any issues with fish sticking to the grill and falling apart is the plank cooking technique. But you don't have to use a thin plank of wood to cook on; some of my best fish is cooked on top of a split log, such as silver birch, ash or cherry, and then surrounded by coals. The coals get the log smouldering at the edges to infuse the fish with delicious smoke and cook it through. Enjoy with a fresh green salad and some new potatoes.

LOG-SMOKED SALMON

FEEDS 4

RECOMMENDED HEAT
moderate

3 lemons

a handful of fresh herbs, such as oregano, thyme or marjoram

1 side of salmon, around 800 g–1 kg/1¾–2¼ lb.

3 tablespoons runny honey

coarse sea salt and freshly ground black pepper

large split hardwood or fruitwood log (big enough for the salmon fillet to sit on)

Set up your barbecue for cooking over moderate heat (150–160°C/300–320°F). Light the charcoal, then add another couple of handfuls and spread it out.

Thinly slice two of the lemons. Place the herbs (reserving a few for the top) and half of the lemon slices on the split log, then place the salmon on top. Season lightly with salt and pepper, and place the remaining lemon slices along the middle of the fillet. Sprinkle over the reserved herbs.

Pop the log with the salmon on top of the coals, close the barbecue lid and cook for 15–20 minutes.

Mix the honey with the juice of the third lemon in a bowl.

Once the internal temperature of the salmon has reached 50°C/122°F on a digital probe thermometer, brush the top with the honey and lemon using a pastry or silicon brush.

Cook for another 8–10 minutes, glazing another two or three times, if you like, until the internal temperature of the thickest part reaches 55°C/131°F.

Using thick heatproof gloves, remove the log from the barbecue and place it on a heatproof surface to serve.

I remember a great trip to Vancouver many years ago, where I enjoyed a treat called Indian candy – basically smoked-cured salmon chunks with a thick glaze of maple syrup on the outside. Absolutely something you can't stop eating. I had some plump trout fillets and decided to recreate Indian candy, but with trout. And it was equally delicious.

MAPLE-GLAZED SMOKED TROUT

FEEDS 2

RECOMMENDED HEAT
low

2 trout or salmon fillets

50 g/scant ¼ cup fine sea salt

50 g/¼ cup demerara/turbinado sugar

6 tablespoons good-quality maple syrup

The night before you plan to smoke the fish, it needs to be lightly cured. Place the trout in a non-reactive bowl. Mix together the salt and sugar, and sprinkle it evenly over the trout. Cover and place in the fridge overnight to cure.

The next morning wipe off any excess salt and sugar.

Set up your barbecue for indirect cooking over low heat (80–100°C/175–210°F), with a chunk or two of cherry wood on the coals for smoke.

Smoke the trout on the barbecue over indirect heat with the lid on for around 30 minutes until the fish reaches an internal temperature of 40°C/104°F on a digital probe thermometer.

Brush over the maple syrup with a pastry or silicon brush and continue to cook for another 30 minutes or so, lightly building up the glaze every few minutes, until the internal temperature of the fish hits 55–60°C/131–140°F.

Remove from the barbecue and rest for as long as you can resist. Serve hot or cold.

I fell in love with tangy zhoug sauce from Yemen after tasting it for the first time. It's kind of a Middle Eastern, herb-rich condiment that has a bit of a kick. It went so well with these charred fresh mackerel.

GRILLED MACKEREL WITH ZHOUG

FEEDS 4

RECOMMENDED HEAT
moderate–high

4 very fresh whole mackerel, cleaned and gutted

1 lemon, quartered

1 quantity Zhoug (see page 112)

sea salt and freshly ground black pepper

4 long, flat metal skewers

Set up your barbecue for direct cooking over moderate–high heat (180–200°C/350–400°F).

Season the mackerel generously with salt and pepper.

Skewer the whole fish on the flat metal skewers (long enough to rest on the edges of the barbecue so the fish is suspended over the grill to prevent it sticking).

Cook the mackerel directly over the heat, turning the skewers every few minutes and squeezing a little of the lemon over the fish, until the skin is crisp and charred and the fish is cooked through with an internal temperature of 55–60°C/131–140°F on a digital probe thermometer.

Serve at once with a drizzle of the zingy zhoug and the remaining lemon quarters for squeezing over.

A large leek can be opened out by cutting it lengthways on one side only, which creates a fantastic wrapper for delicate fish and stops it from sticking to the grill. Here I went for some fresh sea bass, which can be quite delicate and fall apart if it sticks to the grill. Using a leek 'wrapper' adds an extra delicious dimension as the leek chars up.

SEA BASS WRAPPED IN LEEK

FEEDS 2

RECOMMENDED HEAT
moderate–high

1 large leek

1 lemon, thinly sliced

1 sea bass/branzino (about 700 g/1½ lb.), cleaned and gutted, or 2 sea bass/branzino fillets

sea salt and freshly ground black pepper

pre-soaked wooden skewer

Set up your barbecue for indirect cooking over moderate–high heat (180–200°C/350–400°F).

Take the leek and run a sharp knife from top to bottom, only cutting to the middle, not all the way through. Open out the leek sheets.

Stuff a couple of slices of lemon into the cavity of the fish or place them between the fillets if using fillets. Season the skin with salt and pepper.

Wrap a few of the leek sheets around the fish, tucking them in and using the soaked wooden skewer to secure.

Place the fish on the grill (the leek sheets will stop the fish sticking to the grill grate, making it easy to turn). Cook over indirect heat for 20–30 minutes, turning occasionally, until cooked through – it should have an internal temperature of 55–60°C/131–140°F on a digital probe thermometer.

Serve at once.

Monkfish is a great fish to cook on the barbecue using direct grilling. It's firm enough not to fall apart like a lot of the more delicate fish, and, with a spiced crust and a bit of sear, it tastes really special.

BUTTER-SPICED MONKFISH FILLET

FEEDS 2

RECOMMENDED HEAT
moderate

1 monkfish tail (about 450 g/1 lb.), skin and bone removed

30 g/2 tablespoons softened butter

1 teaspoon garam masala or similar spice mix

1 teaspoon cumin seeds

1 teaspoon ground turmeric

1 lemon, quartered

1 tablespoon chopped coriander/cilantro

a pinch of chilli flakes/hot red pepper flakes

Set up your barbecue for two-zone (direct and indirect) cooking at a moderate heat (160–180°C/320–350°F).

Season lightly the outside of the monkfish tail.

Put the softened butter in a bowl, add the spices and squeeze in one of the lemon quarters. Mix to make a spiced butter.

Sear the outside of the monkfish fillet over the coals, then brush on the spiced butter with a pastry or silicon brush. Cook with the barbecue lid on, turning the fish as required during cooking and brushing with a little more butter each time you do so. Once the monkfish is charred, you can move it to a cooler part of the grill and cook over indirect heat until the internal temperature of the monkfish reaches 55–60°C/131–140°F on a digital probe thermometer.

Allow to rest a few minutes, then slice the fish thickly, squeeze over the rest of the lemon quarters and sprinkle with the chopped coriander and chilli flakes.

We're blessed with some wonderful seafood, but many people struggle with cooking it on a barbecue without it sticking and falling apart. In order to stop this, the best tip is to prevent the fish from touching the grate. One of my favourite techniques is to suspend the fish on skewers over the coals.

SEA BREAM WITH CHIMICHURRI ROJO

FEEDS 2

RECOMMENDED HEAT
very high

2 sea bream, cleaned and gutted

1 lemon

sea salt and freshly ground black pepper

CHIMICHURRI ROJO

2 garlic cloves

a handful of freshly chopped flat-leaf parsley and oregano

1 tablespoon dried oregano

60 ml/4 tablespoons extra virgin olive oil, plus extra if needed

a pinch of smoked paprika

2 tablespoons red wine vinegar

1 tablespoon tomato purée/paste

2 long, flat metal skewers

Set up your barbecue for direct cooking, so that you can suspend a couple of long skewers about 15–20 cm/6–8 inches above the embers. A couple of bricks with the coals between them would work at a push. The heat at the cooking level should be hot enough that you can only hold your hand (carefully) at this level for 2–3 seconds (around 200°C/392°F).

Skewer a gutted sea bream onto each skewer, from the mouth down to the tail. Halve the lemon, then cut a slice from each half. Place a slice of lemon inside the cavity of each fish, then thread what's left of the lemon halves onto the ends of the skewers. Season the skin of the fish well with salt and pepper.

Suspend the fish over the coals and cook for 6–7 minutes until the skin crisps and chars slightly, then turn the skewer over and cook the other side for 6–7 minutes until the fish is cooked through – it should have an internal temperature of 55–60°C/131–140°F on a digital probe thermometer.

Make the chimichurri rojo by blitzing up all the ingredients with a good pinch of salt in a food processor or blender until fairly smooth. Loosen it with a little more olive oil, if you wish.

Serve the sea bream with the chimichurro rojo.

I'm a lover of red mullet and I think it's much underrated by a lot of folk. It's a lovely pink, smooth-skinned fish, and the flesh is delicate with a shellfish flavour from all the prawns/shrimp and crustaceans it eats.

I figured it would work well with a red Thai curry coating and a nice crispy, slightly charred skin. This is a lovely way to cook fish as you get a crisp skin, without fear of the fish sticking because it's not in contact with the grill grates.

WHOLE THAI FISH SKEWERS

FEEDS 2

RECOMMENDED HEAT
moderate

2 red mullet, gutted and scaled

2 tablespoons Thai red curry paste

sea salt

coriander/cilantro and lime wedges, to serve

long, flat metal skewers

Set up your barbecue for cooking at a moderate heat (160–180°C/320–350°F), so that the skewered fish can be supported just above the coals.

Skewer the gutted fish through the head, body and out through the tail end. Make a couple of slashes in the thick part of the body to help even cooking, and to allow the curry paste to penetrate the flesh. Season lightly with the salt, and then brush on the Thai red curry paste. Make sure the fish has a nice even coating of the paste.

Place the skewers over the coals and cook, turning occasionally and making sure the char on the skin doesn't get too dark, for 10–12 minutes, or until the thickest part of the fish has an internal temperature of 55°C/130°F on a digital probe thermometer.

Serve on a bed on coriander with lime wedges for squeezing over.

CHAPTER 6

VEGETARIAN

I had been looking for a vegetarian alternative to the ubiquitous pulled pork that was not only acceptable, but really rather fabulous, and I think this pulled fennel is it. When slow-roasted over charcoal and basted with melted butter, sliced fennel becomes sweet and juicy.

PULLED FENNEL & HALLOUMI BURGER

FEEDS 2

RECOMMENDED HEAT
low–moderate

225-g/8-oz. block of halloumi

1 fennel bulb, sliced lengthways to keep the root intact

15 g/1 tablespoon butter

TO SERVE

2 large burger buns

chilli/chili jam

hot chilli/chili sauce (optional)

Set up a barbecue for direct cooking over low-moderate heat (120–150°C/250–300°F). You'll need a lump of pear wood for the smoked halloumi.

Pop a lump of pear wood on the coals (or in a smoker with a lid) to start smoking, then hot-smoke the halloumi for 40 minutes.

Slowly char the fennel bulb for 20–30 minutes until sticky and sweet. Baste the fennel with the butter every now and then. The bulb should fall apart into lovely strands.

Slice the pear-smoked halloumi lengthways down the long edge and pop on the grill next to the fennel until crisp on the outside and soft inside. When cooked well in this way, halloumi loses its squeaky texture and yet stays nice and firm on the grill.

To assemble the burgers, divide the buns between two plates. Add a tablespoon of chilli jam to the bottom half of each bun, spreading to the edges with the back of a spoon. Follow with half of the fennel, one piece of halloumi, an extra dollop of chilli sauce (if you like it hot), and the other half of the bun. Serve immediately.

As halloumi grills over hot coals the surface browns and crisps, intensifying the saltiness of the cheese. Serve with homemade rosemary flatbreads and a fragrant and spicy chermoula drizzled over the top, and you have a real winner.

GRILLED HALLOUMI IN ROSEMARY FLATBREADS

FEEDS 2

RECOMMENDED HEAT
moderate

225-g/8-oz block of halloumi

1 tablespoon olive oil

CHERMOULA

1 red chilli/chile pepper

2 large garlic cloves

a handful of fresh coriander/cilantro, plus extra to serve

6 tablespoons olive oil

2 tablespoons white wine vinegar

juice of 1 lemon

2 teaspoons each paprika and ground cumin

a pinch of sea salt

ROSEMARY FLATBREADS

125 g/1 cup plain/all-purpose flour, plus extra for dusting

75 ml/⅓ cup warm water

½ tablespoon olive oil

½ teaspoon fine sea salt

a sprig of fresh rosemary, leaves removed and finely chopped

Prepare the chermoula by blitzing all the ingredients in a food processor or using a hand blender until you have a loose paste. Add more olive oil, if required, to achieve a spooning consistency.

To prepare the flatbreads, mix all the ingredients together in a bowl, either by hand or using a food mixer with a dough hook, until you have a smooth dough. Knead the dough for 8–10 minutes. Pop the dough in the bowl, cover with clingfilm/plastic wrap, and let rest for 20–30 minutes at room temperature.

Once rested, split the dough into four equal pieces. Dust your work surface with a little flour. Roll the flatbreads into rough rounds using a rolling pin. Bake the flatbreads on the hot grill or hot coals of the barbecue for a few minutes on each side, or until just charred and crisped up in places. Set aside and wrap in a clean kitchen towel to keep warm.

Cut the halloumi block in half horizontally, so you have two large, flat squares. Brush on both sides with olive oil and place on the grill. Cook for around 5–6 minutes, until slightly charred at the edges and golden brown on both sides. Serve on the flatbreads, drizzled with the chermoula.

When vegetables hit the grill, magic happens. As they caramelize, the char adds a lovely smoky sweetness. Here I amplify these flavours by marinating the vegetables in a spicy honey adobo sauce. I had canned chipotles in adobo so used the spicy sauce they come in as the marinade and threaded the chipotles onto the skewers to add that extra something. The honey just helps the caramelization along with a bit of extra sweetness to balance.

VEGETABLES IN ADOBO SKEWERS

FEEDS 2

RECOMMENDED HEAT
moderate–high

a selection of vegetables from the following list: red onion, sweet (bell) peppers, fresh chillies/chiles, mushrooms, courgettes/zucchini, new potatoes

½ x 225-g/8-oz. can chipotle peppers in adobo sauce (about 60 g/2 oz. drained weight)

2 tablespoons runny honey

sea salt and freshly ground black pepper

thin metal skewers

If using potatoes, put these on to par-boil. Meanwhile, prepare the other vegetables as follows: cut the onion into thin wedges, quarter and deseed the peppers, halve the mushrooms and thickly slice the courgette. Drain the potatoes and, when cool enough to handle, slice them into discs, but be careful not to cut them too thin.

In a bowl, mix together the prepared vegetables with the chipotle peppers in adobo sauce, spoon in the honey and season with salt and freshly ground pepper. Stir until the vegetables are coated. Leave to marinate for 1 hour.

Set up barbecue for direct cooking over moderate–high heat (180–200°C/350–400°F).

Thread the vegetables onto your skewers, adding the occasional chipotle pepper in between them. Once your skewers are loaded, place them on the grill and cook for a few minutes on each side until lightly charred and softened.

Enjoy with a cold beer.

Simple but bold flavours are celebrated in this dish. Zhoug (or zhug) is a wonderfully punchy spicy, coriander-rich condiment from Yemen, similar to chimichurri (see page 46). It's completely delicious.

GRILLED VEG WITH ZHOUG

FEEDS 4

RECOMMENDED HEAT
moderate

a selection of veg for grilling, such as sweet (bell) peppers, aubergine/eggplant, courgettes/zucchini, onion and asparagus

1 lemon, halved

3 tablespoons extra virgin olive oil

sea salt and freshly ground black pepper

ZHOUG

a handful of coriander/cilantro (around 30 g/1 oz.)

a small handful of flat-leaf parsley (around 20 g/¾ oz.)

1 green chilli/chile

1 plump garlic clove

1 teaspoon ground cumin

a small pinch of cumin seeds

freshly squeezed juice of ½ lemon

1 teaspoon Aleppo chilli flakes/hot red pepper flakes

80 ml/⅓ cup extra virgin olive oil

Make up the zhoug by blitzing up all the ingredients into a fine sauce using a stick blender or crush them together using a mortar and pestle.

Set up your barbecue for direct cooking at a moderate heat (160–180°C/320–350°F). You could even cook the veg dirty-style directly on the charcoal, if you like.

Start off with the veg that take the longest to cook (onions, courgettes and aubergine) and cut them into 1-cm/½-inch thick circles. Drizzle the cut veg and the lemon halves with a little of the olive oil and season with salt and pepper. Grill them over direct heat until they begin to caramelize and soften.

Add the peppers and finally the asparagus, and continue to cook until all have a nice light charring.

Plate up the veg and drizzle over the zhoug sauce.

I could easily have opted for a chicken satay skewer as it's something of a classic, but I wanted to do something a bit different with the nutty sauce that usually accompanies the chicken, so I decided I should experiment with a 'meaty' miso-marinated aubergine. The results blew me away, so I knew I had to include this recipe in the book.

AUBERGINE SATAY WITH SPICY ALMOND DIPPING SAUCE

FEEDS 2

RECOMMENDED HEAT
moderate–high

1 aubergine/eggplant

1 teaspoon white or red miso paste

1 teaspoon honey

1 teaspoon soy sauce

juice of ½ lime

½ teaspoon mild chilli flakes/red pepper flakes

sea salt and freshly ground black pepper

DIPPING SAUCE

4 teaspoons almond butter

2 tablespoons coconut milk (creamy part at the top of the can)

juice of ½ lime

2 tablespoons sweet chilli/chili sauce

2 teaspoons soy sauce

a pinch of chilli flakes/hot red pepper flakes

pre-soaked small wooden skewers

Cut the aubergine into 2.5-cm/1-inch cubes.

In a bowl mix together the miso paste, honey, soy sauce, lime juice, chill flakes and some salt and pepper. Add the aubergine and let marinate in the fridge for 1–2 hours.

Set up your barbecue for direct cooking over moderate–high heat (180–200°C/350–400°F).

Make up the spicy almond dipping sauce by thoroughly combining the ingredients.

Thread the marinated aubergine cubes onto the soaked wooden skewers, 3 cubes on each.

Grill the skewers for 10–12 minutes, turning occasionally every couple of minutes to build up a nice medium char. The aubergine should start to soften (but don't let it go too soft or the cubes will fall off the skewer). Drizzle with a little of the spicy almond dipping sauce, and place a little sauce by the side to dip the skewers in.

Serve with the dipping sauce on the side.

Bear with me all you meat-lovers… this is really good. I do love a nice steak but, as some of you know, I was a vegetarian for 14 years, and I clearly remember going to barbecues and getting palmed off with dry and lifeless veggie burgers and other vegetarian fare. Usually the most exciting thing on offer would be some grilled vegetable kebabs. Aubergines are wonderful chargrilled over charcoal; they are sponges for flavour and work so well when grilled on the barbecue.

GRILLED AUBERGINE STEAKS WITH MISO & HONEY GLAZE

FEEDS 2

RECOMMENDED HEAT
very high

1 large aubergine/eggplant)

a pinch of chilli flakes/hot red pepper flakes (optional)

sea salt

steamed jasmine rice, to serve

MISO & HONEY GLAZE

1 teaspoon miso paste (any colour will work)

1 teaspoon runny honey

2 teaspoons mirin

1 teaspoon soy sauce

2 teaspoons toasted sesame oil

Set up your barbecue for direct cooking over very high heat (around 200°C/392°F).

Slice the aubergine lengthways into steaks, 2 cm/¾ inch thick. Sprinkle both sides with a little sea salt and let sit on a plate for an hour to remove any bitter juices.

Wipe any excess salt or moisture from the aubergine steaks, and score very slightly with a sharp knife in a criss-cross pattern across both sides.

Mix all the ingredients for the glaze together in a bowl.

Brush the glaze generously over both sides of the steaks, reserving a little of the glaze to brush on at the end.

Cook on the red-hot grill for a few minutes on each side – you're looking for the aubergine to soften a little without becoming mushy and the surface to caramelize nicely without burning. Once softened and nicely charred, brush the steaks with the remaining glaze and sprinkle with a pinch of chilli flakes, if you like.

Serve on a bed of steamed jasmine rice.

Paneer is a very versatile grilling cheese, quite similar to halloumi in that it doesn't melt, it's pretty easy to get hold of the blocks and it's great on skewers. A simple yogurt-based marinade gives a nicely spiced coating, while fresh mint and grilled lime add a little zing. A very easy little skewer to knock out quickly, and so simple to prepare.

TANDOOR-STYLE PANEER SKEWERS

FEEDS 2

RECOMMENDED HEAT
high

3 tablespoons natural/plain yogurt

2 tablespoons tandoori masala spice blend

1 lime, cut in half

1 tablespoon finely chopped mint

a pinch of chilli flakes/hot red pepper flakes

225 g/8 oz. paneer or halloumi cheese, cut into 2-cm/¾-inch cubes

sea salt and freshly ground black pepper

vegetable oil, for oiling the grate

pre-soaked wooden skewers

In a bowl mix the yogurt, tandoori masala spice blend, a quick squeeze of lime juice, the mint, chilli flakes, a pinch of salt and some coarsely ground pepper. Stir until combined.

Put the paneer cubes into the yogurt marinade, stir gently until they are coated in the marinade and leave for a couple of hours in the fridge.

Set up your barbecue for direct cooking over high heat (around 200°C/400°F), with the grill grate in close proximity to the coals.

Thread 3 cubes of paneer onto each soaked skewer.

Oil the grill grate with about 2 teaspoons of vegetable oil, then place the skewers and a lime half onto the grate to grill for a few minutes on each side until starting to char, turning occasionally, with an overall total cooking time of 7–8 minutes.

Squeeze over the juice from the grilled lime to serve.

Chicory (also known as endive) is a wonderful vegetable; it is crisp and refreshing, with a slightly bitter edge. It grills well over a high heat, charring a little and gaining a slightly sweet depth of flavour, while still retaining crispness. Grilled chicory can be eaten in many ways, perhaps served with a creamy sauce or dressed with olive oil and balsamic vinegar. Or accompanied, as here, with a few complementary ingredients, including blue cheese for a bit of salty sharpness. The honey adds just the right sweetness, while the chilli flakes give a little kick of heat for extra interest.

CHARRED CHICORY WITH HONEY, CHILLI & BLUE CHEESE

FEEDS 1

RECOMMENDED HEAT
high

1–2 chicory heads

a drizzle of olive oil

2 tablespoons crumbled blue cheese (such as Roquefort, dolcelatte or Cornish blue)

1 teaspoon runny honey

a pinch of chilli flakes/hot red pepper flakes (optional)

Set up your barbecue for direct cooking over high heat (around 200°C/400°F). Set the grate 2.5–5 cm/ 1–2 inches above the coals.

Cut the chicory into quarters lengthways, keeping the root intact to hold the leaves together.

Drizzle a little olive oil over the chicory leaves, and rub in. Grill the chicory over the hot coals until slightly charred on all sides, turning as required.

Place the chicory in a serving dish. Crumble over the blue cheese, drizzle with the runny honey and sprinkle over the chilli flakes, if you like.

Enjoy the charred chicory alone, or as a great side dish with pork (and many other dishes).

These skewers are simple but have a great flavour and are packed with umami. They are ideal as a side dish or can become the star of the show if you let them shine. Mushrooms are a wonderful blank canvas for soaking up flavours, and they sear beautifully over hot charcoal. My recipe here uses red miso paste, toasted sesame oil and some spicy heat to really make these beautiful mushrooms sing.

MISO & SESAME KING OYSTER MUSHROOMS

FEEDS 2

RECOMMENDED HEAT
moderate–high

1 teaspoon red miso paste

4 tablespoons toasted sesame oil

a pinch of chilli flakes/hot red pepper flakes

3 king oyster mushrooms

sea salt and freshly ground black pepper

very fine metal skewers

Set up your barbecue for direct cooking over moderate–high heat (180–200°C/350–400°F) with the grill grate in close proximity to the coals.

Make up the miso sesame marinade by mixing the miso, sesame oil and chilli flakes in a bowl. Season with a little salt and freshly ground pepper.

Slice the king oyster mushrooms lengthways into 3 slices. Thread onto 2 skewers as shown. Using a silicone pastry brush, paint the marinade onto the surfaces of the mushrooms, and grill for 10–12 minutes until lightly caramelized and the mushrooms are starting to soften, turning halfway through cooking.

If you are yet to try a white barbecue sauce, you might be highly surprised at how good it is. The original, hailing from Alabama, is mayonnaise-based and works so well on smoky chicken or my pulled turkey (see page 78). But the version I've made here goes so well with many vegetable dishes. I went for celeriac 'steaks', as they are a great match for the tangy sauce. Feel free to try other vegetables, such as cauliflower, with this sauce too.

CELERIAC STEAKS WITH WHITE BARBECUE SAUCE

FEEDS 2

RECOMMENDED HEAT
moderate

1 celeriac/celery root

2 tablespoons olive oil

sea salt and freshly ground black pepper

WHITE BARBECUE SAUCE

6 tablespoons mayonnaise

1 tablespoon apple cider vinegar

1 tablespoon pickle juice (from a jar of pickles)

1 teaspoon cream of horseradish

1 teaspoon American mustard

1 teaspoon Worcestershire sauce

½ teaspoon garlic powder

½ teaspoon coarse ground black pepper

½ teaspoon sea salt

½ teaspoon black pepper

¼ teaspoon hot sauce of your choice

Set up your barbecue for direct cooking at a moderate heat (around 160–180°C/320–350°F).

Make up the white barbecue sauce by mixing the ingredients together with 1 tablespoon of water until you have a rich, creamy and tangy sauce.

Remove the outer skin of the celeriac and cut it into steaks around 1 cm/½ inch thick. Pour over the olive oil and rub it into the celeriac steaks. Season with salt and pepper.

Place the celeriac steaks on the grill and cook with the lid on, turning occasionally, for 12–15 minutes until they have seared slightly, are a lovely caramel colour in places and have softened.

Plate up the celeriac steaks and drizzle over the white barbecue sauce. Serve at once.

So I've been playing with my food again… I'm especially fond of veg from which you can create a 'steak' (such as cauliflower and celeriac, see recipe opposite) to be grilled and topped with all sorts of exciting flavours. The taste of charred cauliflower with the bold flavours of kimchi and mature Cheddar surprised me with how well it worked. And I love surprises! In this recipe I have gone with a beetroot kimchi, but this will work well with any variety of kimchi.

KIMCHEESE CAULIFLOWER SLICES

FEEDS 21

RECOMMENDED HEAT
moderate

1 cauliflower

2 tablespoons cold-pressed rapeseed oil

8 tablespoons beetroot/beet kimchi or other kimchi

100 g/1 cup grated mature/ sharp Cheddar cheese

Set up your barbecue for two-zone (direct and indirect) grilling at a moderate heat (150–160°C/300–320°F).

Slice the cauliflower into 4 thick steaks, from the top of the cauliflower to the bottom. You'll end up with 2 wider steaks (from the middle of the cauliflower) and 2 smaller steaks (from the edges).

Rub the oil all over the cauliflower steaks and place them on the grill. Cook over direct heat for 12–15 minutes, watching that they don't burn (a little char is ok, but if they char too quickly, move them to the indirect side of the grill).

Once the cauliflower is charred and softened, spoon 2 tablespoons kimchi on to each cauliflower steak, then sprinkle the grated Cheddar cheese over the top.

Pop them back onto the indirect side of the grill, and cook for another 4–5 minutes with the lid on until the cheese has melted.

This is a wonderful vegetarian alternative to the chorizo sausage rafts on page 46. They are equally delicious with the charred leeks smothered with melted Cheddar cheese and chimichurri. A truly delicious combination.

CHARRED LEEK RAFTS

FEEDS 2

RECOMMENDED HEAT
moderate

6 leeks

1 teaspoon extra virgin olive oil

a handful of grated mature/sharp Cheddar cheese or vegan cheese

sea salt and freshly ground black pepper

CHIMICHURRI

2 garlic cloves

a handful of flat-leaf parsley and oregano

1 tablespoon dried oregano

a pinch of smoked paprika

60 ml/4 tablespoons extra virgin olive oil

2 tablespoons red wine vinegar

1 tablespoon Aleppo chilli flakes/ hot red pepper flakes

pre-soaked wooden skewers

Set up your barbecue for direct cooking over moderate heat (160–180°C/320–350°F).

Trim the leeks, then place them next to each other and use the soaked wooden skewers to make a raft with the leeks, skewering through the leeks close to either end.

Rub the olive oil over the leeks, lightly season with a pinch of salt and pepper and place on the grill. Cook for 8–10 minutes with the lid on until the outside of the leeks has charred slightly and they have softened.

While the leeks are cooking, blitz up all the chimichurri ingredients with a couple of good pinches of sea salt in a food processor or blender.

Place the cheese on top of the leeks, then close the barbecue lid again and cook for a few minutes until the cheese has melted. Drizzle over a couple of teaspoons of the chimichurri and serve.

Paella of sorts is a firm family favourite with my clan. It's certainly never a traditional paella, but something simpler. This recipe is vegan, but a few grilled chicken thighs and pan-fried chorizo chunks can be added separately for those who like meat. Or perhaps some grilled prawns/shrimp?

SPANISH RICE WITH GRILLED PADRÓN PEPPERS

FEEDS 8

RECOMMENDED HEAT
moderate

4 tablespoons extra virgin olive oil

2 onions, finely chopped

2 cloves garlic, finely chopped

1 red (bell) pepper, chopped

1 yellow (bell) pepper, chopped

1 green (bell) pepper, chopped

2 tablespoons smoked paprika

750 g/4 cups paella rice

a pinch of saffron, soaked in
2 tablespoons hot water

3 litres/12 cups hot vegetable stock

1 lemon, cut into 8 wedges

a handful of freshly chopped
flat-leaf parsley

200 g/7 oz. padrón peppers

sea salt and freshly ground black
pepper

paella pan or similar large flat pan
that will fit in your barbecue with the
lid down

Set up your barbecue for direct cooking at a moderate heat (around 150°C/300°F).

Place the paella pan over the heat and add the olive oil, onions, garlic and peppers, and cook for about 10 minutes until the onions have softened and are lightly caramelized. Add the paprika and stir. Add a couple of pinches of salt and ground black pepper.

Add the rice and cook for 4–5 minutes to toast the grains and coat them in oil. Add the saffron with the soaking water, followed by 1 litre/4 cups of the stock. Pop the barbecue lid on and cook for 10 minutes until most of the stock has been absorbed.

Add another 1 litre/4 cups of stock and cook for a further 10 minutes, then add the final 1 litre/4 cups of stock and cook for around 15 minutes until all of the stock has been absorbed.

Top the rice with the lemon wedges and sprinkle over the flat-leaf parsley. Remove the pan from the heat and set aside to rest.

Grill the padrón peppers directly over the coals until slightly charred, blistered and starting to soften. Place the charred padrón peppers on top of the rice and serve.

CHAPTER 7

SALADS, SIDES & SAUCES

In addition to good bread, I think you need something tangy to cut through rich, fatty barbecue food – as a cornerstone to an outdoor feast. A simple coleslaw does the job perfectly and is always good to have at hand when you're throwing a barbecue. Homemade coleslaw is also fresh and not as creamy and gloopy as commercial coleslaw.

SIMPLE COLESLAW

FEEDS 8

2–3 large carrots

½ celeriac/celery root

½ small red cabbage

4 heaped tablespoons good-quality mayonnaise

2 teaspoons American yellow mustard

4 tablespoons freshly squeezed lemon juice

sea salt and freshly ground black pepper

Peel and coarsely grate the carrots and celeriac. Thinly slice the red cabbage into ribbons – get these as thin as you can. Mix the vegetables together in a large bowl.

Mix all the liquid ingredients together in a separate bowl, and then stir through the vegetables.

Season with sea salt and black pepper to taste – a pinch of each should be about right.

Grilling the carrots, celeriac and red cabbage I've used for this recipe before grating them gives the finished coleslaw a very different taste and texture to a regular simple coleslaw (see recipe opposite), but it works really nicely with a spicy hit from the piri piri hot sauce. I like to serve this as a side with the Quick Sosaties lamb skewers on page 40 – it makes a really tasty accompaniment and is quick to pull together.

GRILLED VEG PIRI PIRI SLAW

FEEDS 2

RECOMMENDED HEAT
moderate–high

2 carrots, peeled and halved lengthways

¼ celeriac/celery root

¼ red cabbage

1 tablespoon olive oil

3 tablespoons good-quality mayonnaise

3 tablespoons freshly squeezed lemon juice

2 teaspoons piri piri sauce

sea salt and freshly ground black pepper

Set up your barbecue for close proximity direct cooking over moderate–high heat (180–200°C/ 350–400°F).

Prepare the vegetables, rub the oil over them and place them on the grill – you're aiming for a quick char for flavour rather than cooking them through, so a couple of minutes on each side on a hot grill should do this perfectly.

Allow to cool, then, using a food processor, grate the carrot and celeriac. Finely shred the red cabbage using a sharp knife. Place all the veg in a bowl.

Mix together the mayonnaise, lemon juice and piri piri sauce. Pour this mixture over the vegetables, stir to ensure everything is evenly coated, and season with salt and black pepper.

When running barbecue classes at my UK BBQ School, I often change my dishes around. One of my recent inclusions has proven to be a real hit, and so many people just can't get enough of these chimichurri roasties and ask for the recipe, so here it is! These could be a side, but just a bowl of these by themselves is a feast.

CHIMICHURRI ROASTIES

FEEDS 4

RECOMMENDED HEAT
moderate

1 kg/2¼ lb. baby/new potatoes

4 tablespoons extra virgin olive oil

sea salt and freshly ground black pepper

CHIMICHURRI

2 garlic cloves

80 ml/⅓ cup extra virgin olive oil

2 teaspoons red wine vinegar

2 tablespoons dried oregano

2 tablespoons Aleppo chilli flakes/ hot red pepper flakes

a small handful of oregano or marjoram

a good handful of flat-leaf parsley

sea salt

heavy-duty roasting pan

Par-boil the potatoes for around 10 minutes until soft (check with the point of a sharp knife). Drain.

Blitz up all the chimichurri ingredients with a couple of good pinches of sea salt in a food processor or blender.

Set up your barbecue for direct cooking over moderate heat (160–180°C/320–350°F). You can also cook the roasties in an open fire grill, firepit or wood-fired oven.

Place the potatoes in the heavy-duty roasting pan, drizzle over the olive oil and season with a good pinch of coarse sea salt and black pepper.

Place the roasting pan on the barbecue directly over the coals. The roasties will start to crisp up after 20–30 minutes, depending on the exact temperature of your coals.

Once the potatoes are nicely crisp and maybe a little charred in places, spoon over the chimichurri and serve hot.

My kids are always asking for hasselback potatoes these days; they love the crispy outside texture and soft insides when you cook them on the barbecue. I'm always looking for different toppings to make them a bit more fun. The melted cheese and crispy onion topping went down very well, with the cheese oozing into the gaps between the potato slices.

CHEESE-&-ONION-TOPPED HASSELBACK POTATOES

FEEDS 4

RECOMMENDED HEAT
high

8 potatoes, all a similar size

2 tablespoons olive oil

200 g/2 cups grated melting cheese, such as Cheddar or a firm mozzarella

4 tablespoons crispy onion flakes

sea salt and freshly ground black pepper

Set up your barbecue for indirect cooking at a high heat (around 200°C/400°F). You can also use a wood-fired oven.

Place two wooden spoons on a chopping board and place a potato in-between the handles. Using a sharp knife, cut down into the potato, using the spoon handles to stop you cutting all the way through. Continue slicing every 3 mm/⅛ inch to create the hasselback effect. Repeat for all of the potatoes.

Drizzle the potatoes with the olive oil and rub it in. Season generously with sea salt and black pepper.

Place the potatoes on the barbecue and cook them over indirect heat with the lid on for around 40 minutes until the outside is crispy and the potatoes are cooked through.

Sprinkle the cheese on top followed by the crispy onion flakes, then cook with the lid on for a further 5 minutes until the cheese has melted.

You could say that I'm a little bit obsessed with 'nduja! This spicy, spreadable, pork-fat salami is a true revelation when you first try it – and very addictive. Fortunately my mate Marc Dennis at Duchy Charcuterie in Cornwall makes the best I've ever tasted. The way it melts when slightly warmed and releases its spicy fat over these hasselback potatoes, running down into the space between the slices, is just sublime.

'NDUJA-TOPPED HASSELBACK POTATOES

FEEDS 4

RECOMMENDED HEAT
high

8 potatoes, all roughly the same size

2 tablespoons olive oil

4 tablespoons 'nduja

2 spring onions/scallions, chopped

sea salt and freshly ground black pepper

Set up your barbecue for indirect cooking at a high heat (around 200°C/400°F). You can also use a wood-fired oven.

Place two wooden spoons on a chopping board and place a potato in-between the handles. Using a sharp knife, cut down into the potato, using the spoon handles to stop you cutting all the way through. Continue slicing every 3 mm/⅛ inch to create the hasselback effect. Repeat for all of the potatoes.

Drizzle the potatoes with the olive oil and rub it in. Season generously with sea salt and black pepper.

Place the potatoes on the barbecue and cook them over indirect heat with the lid on for around 40 minutes until the outside is crispy and the potatoes are cooked through.

Serve the potatoes topped with the 'nduja and chopped spring onions.

There's a recipe that a lot of the barbecue community do called an ABT (Atomic Buffalo Turd), not the nicest of names... but a truly delicious treat. It's a cream cheese-stuffed jalapeño wrapped in bacon and then smoked until the jalapeño flesh is soft and caramelized. I had some wonderful fresh jalapeños sent to me by a friend who runs the Upton Cheney Chilli farm and they were perfect for this. Here I've chosen prosciutto instead of bacon.

STUFFED JALAPEÑO SKEWERS

FEEDS 4 (side or starter)

RECOMMENDED HEAT moderate

200 g/1 cup minus 2 tablespoons full-fat cream cheese

a handful of chives, chopped

8 fresh jalapeño peppers

8 slices of prosciutto

sea salt

pre-soaked short wooden skewers

Set up your barbecue for direct cooking over moderate heat (around 180°C/350°F) with the grill grate in close proximity to the coals.

Put the cream cheese in a bowl, add the chives and a pinch of salt and stir until combined.

Slice through each chilli/chile lengthways from the tip but not fully in half. Use the tip of your knife to remove the white ribs inside and some of the seeds. Use a teaspoon to spoon in the cream cheese and chive mixture to fill each pepper. Wrap a slice of prosciutto around it to create a sealed package. Thread 2 stuffed peppers onto a skewer, and repeat until all the chillies are used.

Place the skewers on the grill over the embers and cook for 8–10 minutes, turning occasionally until the prosciutto is crispy and the jalapeños charred and softened.

Enjoy with a cold beer.

Aubergine is a wonderful blank canvas, but when seared and charred over flames, it takes on a delicious smokiness that is hard to beat and it is used in plenty of Middle Eastern-style dishes.

This is a very adaptable recipe which you can take in different directions, such as using baharat or ras el hanout spice mix to change things up. However, this simple approach is very tasty and well worth trying.

TURKISH CHILLI AUBERGINE SKEWER

FEEDS 4

RECOMMENDED HEAT
moderate–high

2 aubergines/eggplants, cut into 2.5-cm/1-inch cubes (I used graffiti ones for their lovely stripes)

3 tablespoons olive oil

3 tablespoons Aleppo chilli flakes/hot red pepper flakes

sea salt and freshly ground black pepper

natural/plain yogurt and tahini, to serve

thin, flat metal skewers

Set up your barbecue for direct cooking over moderate–high heat (180–200°C/350–400°F).

Put the aubergine cubes in a bowl. Drizzle over the olive oil and roll the cubes around in the oil to coat. Sprinkle over the chilli flakes evenly and season with salt and freshly ground pepper.

Slide the aubergine cubes onto thin flat metal skewers, and grill for 14–16 minutes until slightly charred and the aubergine softens.

Perfect finished with a drizzle of yogurt and tahini over the top.

'My name is Marcus and I'm an 'nduja addict.' I just can't get enough of this spicy spreadable salami from Calabria. These skewers can be enjoyed as a side dish or as the main star of the show – I found I just couldn't stop eating them, so how you enjoy it is up to you, just give it a go.

'NDUJA BUTTER-BASTED CABBAGE SKEWERS

FEEDS 4

RECOMMENDED HEAT
moderate–high

½ red cabbage, cut into wedges 3 cm/1¼ inch thick

½ white cabbage, cut into wedges 3 cm/1¼ inch thick

sea salt and freshly ground black pepper

BUTTER BASTE
30 g/1 oz. 'nduja

30 g/2 tablespoons butter

large double-pronged skewers

Set up your barbecue for direct cooking over moderate–high heat (180–200°C/350–400°F) with the hot coals close to the grill grate.

Push the skewers through the sides of the cabbage slabs, a couple of chunks of cabbage per skewer. (The prongs on the skewers will stop the cabbage falling apart as it cooks.)

Warm the 'nduja and butter in a small pan until melted.

Season the cabbage with salt and pepper on both sides and place over the charcoal to char, with the skewers in close proximity to the coals; this will take 12–14 minutes.

Once you get a nice char on the edges of the cabbage, use a pastry or silicone brush to start basting with the 'nduja butter, lightly but evenly. Be careful as this added fat can start flaring up as it drips onto the coals. Turn the cabbage every few minutes and keep basting until all the baste is used up, then cook for a couple of minutes on each side until the cabbage has really softened up.

Serve while still hot.

This recipe is so tasty and works wonderfully as an appetizer, but it makes a great side dish too, perhaps with some naan and a dhal. The key is to get some crispy charred edges and for the cabbage to soften as you baste it with the delicious spiced butter. For a vegan alternative swap the butter for an additional 4–5 tablespoons rapeseed oil.

GRILLED SWEETHEART CABBAGE TOPPED WITH SPICED BUTTER & ALMONDS

FEEDS 2

RECOMMENDED HEAT
moderate

2 tablespoons flaked/sliced almonds

1 sweetheart cabbage

1 tablespoon rapeseed oil

50 g/3½ tablespoons softened salted butter

1 teaspoon Kashmiri or tandoori masala powder

1 teaspoon ground turmeric

1 teaspoon ground cumin

1 teaspoon Aleppo chilli flakes/hot red pepper flakes

sea salt and freshly ground black pepper

small cast-iron or other heavy-duty pan

Set up your barbecue for lid-on direct cooking at a moderate heat (160–180°C/320–350°F).

Lightly toast the flaked almonds in the small pan over the coals and set aside. Coarsely chop the almonds once cool.

Cut the cabbage in half lengthways, brush it lightly with the rapeseed oil and season lightly, then place on the grill. Cook for 10–15 minutes until the edges are charred.

Meanwhile, make a spiced butter to baste over it. Mix together the softened butter, Kashmiri or tandoori masala powder, turmeric and cumin until combined.

Once the cabbage is nicely charred, start to brush the spiced butter onto the cut side of the cabbage with a pastry or silicone brush. Continue to cook for 5–6 minutes, brushing with the butter every couple of minutes. You should see the cabbage start to soften.

Sprinkle with the chilli flakes and chopped toasted almonds and lightly season to taste. Serve at once

FEEDS 6

RECOMMENDED HEAT
moderate–high

1 red onion, diced

1 garlic clove, finely chopped

1 red (bell) pepper, cored, deseeded, and diced

1 tablespoon sunflower oil

1 kg/2¼ lb. smoked beef brisket (or pork) leftovers, cubed

400-g/14-oz. can pinto beans, drained

2 x 400-g/14-oz. cans butter/lima beans, drained

1 kg/2¼ lb. passta/strained tomatoes

4 tablespoons tomato ketchup

4 tablespoons barbecue sauce

2 tablespoons barbecue dry rub (just use your favourite)

1 tablespoon American yellow mustard

3 tablespoons cider vinegar

3 tablespoons maple syrup

1 tablespoon packed soft brown sugar

2 teaspoons hot sauce (such as Tabasco or similar)

sea salt and freshly ground black pepper

crisp-skinned baked potatoes, to serve (optional)

Dutch oven or cast-iron or heavy-duty pan

If you're cooking lots of barbecue meats, you'll no doubt have leftovers at some point, so having a reliable barbecue beans recipe is a godsend. You can mix this up to suit your needs and riff off the basic recipe as you please. These campfire beans are a family favourite for using up leftover beef short ribs, pulled pork and pork belly, or in this case, smoked beef brisket. Cooked in a Dutch oven or lidded flameproof dish over a firepit, you can leave this recipe ticking over for hours.

BARBECUE CAMPFIRE BEANS

Set up your barbecue or firepit for direct cooking over flames at moderate–high heat (180–200°C/350–400°F).

Soften the onion, garlic and pepper in the oil in a Dutch oven or cast-iron pan over the moderate-hot fire for 10 minutes.

Add the cubed brisket or pork, and cook for a further 10 minutes.

Add the remainder of the ingredients, season to taste, and stir. Let cook for at least a couple of hours, preferably 4 hours, with the pan lid on. Stir occasionally and top up with water or beer if the mixture gets too dry. Once cooked, the meat should be falling apart and tender, and the sauce nice and thick.

Enjoy your campfire beans on top of baked potatoes, or in a million other ways – the choice is yours.

I've been reducing the amount of carbs I've been eating for the last couple of years, and this recipe has been one of my favourite things to make. Personally I think it is even tastier with celeriac than potato, and even better with a touch of smoke.

SMOKY CELERIAC DAUPHINOISE

FEEDS 2

RECOMMENDED HEAT
moderate

1 celeriac/celery root

1 garlic clove, finely chopped

200 ml/scant 1 cup double/ heavy cream

200 ml/scant 1 cup full-fat/ whole milk

15 g/1 tablespoons butter

sea salt and freshly ground black pepper

cast-iron or heavy-duty pan

Set up your barbecue for indirect cooking at a moderate heat (around 160°C/320°F), with a chunk of light smoking wood, such as cherry wood, on the coals.

Remove the skin from the celeriac with a peeler or sharp knife and remove any parts of the root. Cut the celeriac in half from the top through the middle, then slice it into thin half-moon slices (as thin as you can get with a very sharp knife).

Lay the sliced celeriac in the pan, sprinkle over the finely chopped garlic and pour over the cream and milk. Add the butter to the top and season with a good pinch of salt and pepper.

Place on the barbecue and cook over indirect heat with the lid on for about 40 minutes until cooked through, ensuring the pan doesn't burn or run dry. The celeriac should be nice and soft, the creamy sauce reduced and the top lovely and brown.

Coconut is awesome and adds a lovely creaminess to this spicy salsa. You can vary which type of chilli you use to tailor the heat to suit your palate, so I opted for a mix of habanero and jalapeño. This salsa goes well with plenty of the dishes in this book, the Caribbean-inspired ones in particular, such as the Coconut Curry Monkfish on page 93.

SPICY LIME & COCONUT SALSA

FEEDS 2

80 g/2¾ oz. fresh coconut flesh, plus a few chunks to garnish

freshly squeezed juice of ½ a lime

2 tablespoons coconut milk

1 tablespoon finely chopped fresh red chilli/chile of your choice

sea salt

Prepare the fresh coconut by blitzing it in a food processor until finely shredded.

Place the coconut in a bowl, pour over the lime juice and add the coconut milk.

Season with salt and stir in most of the chopped chilli, reserving a little to garnish.

Top off with the reserved chilli and add a couple of chunks of coconut on top before serving.

This fruity, zingy yet creamy salsa is a wonderful accompaniment to rich meaty skewers.

MANGO & AVOCADO SALSA

FEEDS 2

1 ripe avocado

½ ripe mango

juice of ½ lime (reserve the other ½ lime to serve)

2 banana shallots, finely diced

a small handful of fresh coriander/cilantro leaves, finely chopped

sea salt

Peel and stone/pit both the avocado and mango and dice up the flesh. Drop the flesh into a mixing bowl and squeeze over the lime juice.

Add the shallots along with a pinch of salt and the finely chopped coriander.

Transfer to a serving bowl, along with the lime quarters to squeeze over if you want it to be a bit more zingy.

Grilling the pineapple for this salsa gives lovely caramel notes; don't grill the pineapple for a fresher zingy taste.

PINEAPPLE SALSA

FEEDS 2

RECOMMENDED HEAT
high

100 g/3½ oz. fresh pineapple

freshly squeezed juice of ½ a lime

2 tablespoons finely chopped coriander/cilantro

2 tablespoons finely chopped mint

1 tablespoons finely chopped fresh chilli/chile of your choice

sea salt

If you want to grill the pineapple, set up your barbecue for direct cooking over high heat (around 200°C/400°F).

Cook the pineapple over the hot charcoal for 8–10 minutes and allow it to cool down before chopping it finely. Alternatively, use the fresh pineapple as it comes and again chop finely.

Either way, simply combine the pineapple with the rest of the ingredients in a bowl, season with salt and stir to mix.

I love to tinker with combinations of ingredients for sauces, glazes and marinades. Often you place two ingredients together and they just work in harmony. I found that with the sweetness of peaches and the smoky heat of chipotle. I went for super easy to prep for this, opting for canned peach slices and chipotle chillies in adobo sauce. Leave out the mayonnaise if you just want to make a salsa.

PEACH & CHIPOTLE MAYO

FEEDS 2

80 g/3 oz. canned peach slices in syrup (reserve 2 tablespoons of the syrup)

40 g/1½ oz. canned chipotle chillies/chiles in adobo sauce (drained weight)

5 tablespoons good-quality mayonnaise

Set aside one of the peach slices and half a chipotle.

Place the remaining peach slices and chipotles into a jug/pitcher and blend with a stick blender, then add the reserved peach syrup.

Stir through the mayo and spoon into a serving bowl.

Finely chop the reserved peach slice and chipotle half and scatter the pieces over the top of the bowl to serve.

A good mayonnaise recipe is a wonderful thing to have in your barbecue repertoire. I like to add an extra element to my mayonnaise by using the whole egg and charred woody herbs.

TOASTED HERB MAYONNAISE

FEEDS 4

6–8 sprigs of rosemary or thyme (or a combination of both)

1 large/US extra-large egg

240 ml/1 cup light olive oil

1 tablespoon freshly squeezed lemon juice

sea salt

heatproof mortar and pestle

Place the herbs in a heatproof mortar and toast the herbs with a blow torch or a chunk of hot charcoal. Then use the pestle to grind the herbs to a fine powder.

In a tall narrow jug/pitcher, place the egg, oil, lemon juice and a pinch of salt. Using a stick blender, blitz until it forms a thick and creamy mayonnaise. Pour the mayonnaise into the mortar and stir to combine the toasted herbs.

Store covered in the fridge for up to 2 days.

Fats, oils and salts are great carriers of flavour, and toasted herbs are particularly wonderful flavours to carry onto your meats, fish or vegetables.

CHARRED HERB OIL

MAKES 125 ML/½ CUP

a few sprigs of woody herbs, such as rosemary, thyme or bay

2 teaspoons coarse sea salt

100 ml/scant ½ cup olive oil

Place the herbs and salt into a heat-resistant bowl and then carefully place a lump of hot lumpwood charcoal or a hardwood/fruitwood ember on top of the herbs. They should release a fragrant smoke and go slightly charred and crispy after a few minutes.

Remove the charcoal and use a mortar and pestle to crunch up the herbs and salt. Add the olive oil and leave to infuse for 2 hours.

You can leave the herbs in or strain them out. Store covered in the fridge for up to 1 week.

I love chimichurri, and it can come in many different variations, including the slightly sweeter chimichurri rojo. It's great as a condiment in itself, but here I mix it with butter.

CHIMICHURRI ROJO BUTTER

MAKES 340 G/1½ CUPS

RECOMMENDED HEAT
moderate

1 mini sweet red pepper

2 garlic cloves

2 good pinches sea salt

80 ml/⅓ cup extra virgin olive oil

2 teaspoons red wine vinegar

2 tablespoons dried oregano

2 tablespoons Aleppo chilli flakes/hot red pepper flakes

a small handful of oregano or marjoram

a good handful of flat-leaf parsley

200 g/1¾ stick softened butter

Set up your barbecue for direct cooking over moderate heat (around 160°C/320°F).

Char the sweet mini red pepper directly over the coals for a few minutes to char slightly and soften. Remove the stem and core/seeds.

Place the pepper in a jug/pitcher with all the remaining ingredients except the butter, and blitz up with a stick blender to a coarse paste.

Mix the chimichurri with the softened butter, then wrap in clingfilm/plastic wrap to make a sausage shape and place in the fridge to set.

To use, cut circles of the chimichurri rojo butter and add to grilled vegetables, fish or meats.

Store wrapped in the fridge for up to 2 days.

Maple chilli butter provides a simple way to pep up the flavour of grilled veg, a plump crispy pork chop or even popcorn.

MAPLE CHILLI BUTTER

MAKES 75 G/5 TABLESPOONS

60 g/4 tablespoons softened butter

2 teaspoons maple syrup

2 teaspoons Aleppo chilli flakes/hot red pepper flakes

Mix all the ingredients together thoroughly in a bowl.

Cover and keep in the fridge for as long as you can resist.

Adding a hint of smoke to an oil adds a lick of extra flavour to all sorts of food. I always find it a useful thing to have handy; I add to salads and grilled veg, and it's just wonderful drizzled over pizza. You could try dipping bread in it. The process is quite simple, and you can choose the wood embers, or just use charcoal, to vary the flavours the oil takes on. The chilli flakes just give a wonderful colour and a bit of heat, so choose your chilli variety wisely.

SMOKY CHILLI OIL

**MAKES 110 ML/
SCANT ½ CUP**

100 ml/scant ½ cup light olive oil

2 teaspoons Aleppo chilli flakes/hot red pepper flakes

Place the olive oil and Aleppo chilli flakes into a heat-resistant bowl.

Take an ember of hardwood, fruitwood or lumpwood charcoal – I went for a sweet smoky chunk of cherry ember – and carefully place it in the oil. It should start to smoke.

Cover the bowl snugly with a sheet of foil and leave for about 10 minutes; the foil will trap the smoke, which infuses into the oil.

Have a taste of the oil, and repeat if you want a smokier flavour. Leave to mellow overnight in a covered bowl.

Store covered in the fridge for up to 1 week.

CHAPTER 8

SWEET
THINGS

This is such a wonderfully easy recipe with an indulgent Middle Eastern feel. I absolutely love fresh figs cooked in or over coals and here they are popped on skewers and charred over hot coals with a little honey. Serve with toasted pistachio kernels, an extra drizzle of honey and a dollop of creamy mascarpone for a simple dessert with real wow factor.

FIGS WITH HONEY & PISTACHIOS

FEEDS 2

RECOMMENDED HEAT
moderate–high

40 g/⅓ cup shelled pistachios

4 fresh figs

2 tablespoons runny honey

2 heaped tablespoons mascarpone

pre-soaked bamboo skewers

Set up your barbecue for direct cooking over moderate–high heat (180–200°C/350–400°F). Make sure the grill grate is in close proximity to the embers.

Toast the pistachios in a pan over the heat until lightly browned, then coarsely chop them and set aside.

Cut each fig in half lengthways and thread the halves onto the skewers. Place on the grill. After a couple of minutes the figs will start to caramelize.

Drizzle over 1 teaspoon of the runny honey and cook for a minute or so more, but don't let the figs get too soft as they cook.

Plate up the skewers with the mascarpone, drizzle over the remaining honey and sprinkle over the toasted pistachios.

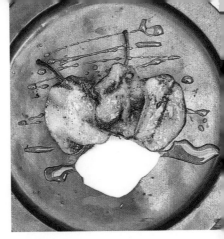

I wondered whether I would get this recipe past the book's editor, as it is ridiculously simple. However, it is so delicious that I just couldn't leave it out. I'm very glad I did include it. When I was writing this book, the pears in my garden were plentiful. Pears are at their best when charred slightly over direct heat, while the little drizzle of honey turns them into something that is almost like candied pear, but with smoke and char.

GRILLED PEARS WITH HONEY

FEEDS 2

RECOMMENDED HEAT
high

2 pears (ideally, sweet Comice-style pears)

2 tablespoons runny honey

cream or plain/natural yogurt, to serve

Set up your barbecue for direct cooking over high heat (around 200°C/400°F).

Cut each pear into four slices lengthways (they don't need to be peeled first, nor cored).

Place the pear slices on the grill over direct heat to sear and caramelize. Sear one side first, then drizzle the slices evenly with honey before flipping and drizzling again on the other side; this should take a few minutes for each side. You'll know when the pears are cooked because the flesh starts to soften and the honey caramelizes into a toffee-like crust.

The pears are perfect served with a little cream or yogurt.

Grilling fruit is wonderful, and a touch of caramelization is magic. Here the fire brings out an unexpected jamminess in the strawberries, completely transforming them. This classic Eton Mess combination provides a great pairing with a contrast of textures and flavours – sweet, crunchy and creamy. Skewering the strawberries makes them easier to control, otherwise it can be like herding cats.

GRILLED STRAWBERRY ETON MESS

FEEDS 2

RECOMMENDED HEAT
moderate–high

2 ready-made meringue nests

12 strawberries

2 tablespoons extra-thick double/heavy cream

a few mint leaves, finely chopped

pre-soaked wooden skewers

Set up your barbecue for direct cooking over moderate–high heat (180–200°C/350–400°F). Make sure the grill grate is in close proximity to the embers.

Smash up the meringues (place them in a plastic bag to keep the pieces from going everywhere).

Place 3 strawberries on each wooden skewer and place on the grill. Grill the skewers until the fruit just starts to char and soften, around 2–3 minutes per side. Remove from the grill before they get too soft and fall off the skewer.

Prepare 2 plates with the crushed meringue and a dollop of the cream. Place the strawberry skewers on the meringue and sprinkle the chopped mint over the top. You can then dip the strawberries into the cream and meringue. Heaven.

Stone fruits, such as peaches, are a great way to end a meal of rich barbecue food – they are light and zingy, and can refresh a jaded palate. They are wonderful grilled, but I love them cooked simply on the barbecue or in a cast-iron pan in a wood-fired oven. There's no need to be fancy here: as simple things go, these are sublime. The pumpkin seeds offer a nice element of toasty crunch.

CAST-IRON PEACHES

FEEDS 2

RECOMMENDED HEAT
moderate

2 perfectly ripe peaches, halved and stoned/pitted

2 teaspoons demerara/turbinado sugar

2 tablespoons pumpkin seeds

a few thyme leaves

cream or ice cream, to serve

cast-iron or heavy-duty frying pan/skillet

Set up your barbecue for direct cooking over moderate heat (around 180°C/350°F) or heat a wood-fired oven to around 200°C/400°F.

Place the peach halves, cut-side up, in a cast-iron frying pan. Sprinkle the sugar evenly over the cut surface, then dust with the pumpkin seeds and thyme leaves.

Cook the peaches on the barbecue with the lid on (in the wood-fired oven) for around 15–20 minutes, turning them halfway through the cooking time, or until the peaches soften and the tops are charred and caramelized. Make sure the pumpkin seeds don't burn, but just toast off.

Serve warm with your choice of cream or ice cream.

Grown-ups can enjoy lollipops too with these tasty charred pineapple skewers, basted in a sweet rum butter that packs them with Caribbean flavour. Enjoy with friends as the perfect finale to a summer barbecue – and if you do want to share them with the kids, simply omit the rum!

RUM BUTTER-BASTED PINEAPPLE LOLLIPOPS

FEEDS 4

RECOMMENDED HEAT
high

30 g/2 tablespoons butter

2 tablespoons demerara/turbinado sugar

25–50 ml/1–2 oz. rum, to taste

4 round slices of fresh pineapple, each about 2-cm/¾-inch thick, skin cut away

pre-soaked bamboo skewers

Set up your barbecue for direct cooking over high heat (around 200°C/400°F).

Mix together all the ingredients (except the pineapple) in a small metal bowl and pop it next to the coals to warm up. Once the butter has melted, stir to combine.

Thread the pineapple slices onto your skewers to make lollipops and then grill over hot coals until starting to char and caramelize, turning occasionally.

Start brushing the sweet rum butter over the pineapple using a pastry or silicone brush to build up a caramelized glaze. The pineapple should have started to soften too.

Once charred and softened, you can take them off the heat and eat just like a lollipop! Who said the kids have all the fun?

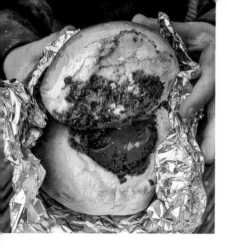

My kids go crazy for this recipe, and it's as simple as you can get. My wife and I like to make sure we get one as well. A cottage bread roll (a traditional style of roll that originated in England) makes the ideal container for the oozing melted chocolate: the little top knot pulls off easily, then you can scoop out the bread, fill with chocolate hazelnut spread, and pop the top back on. This can be achieved with other bread rolls by cutting into the top, but is less elegant.

CAMPFIRE CHOCOLATE ROLLS

FEEDS 4

RECOMMENDED HEAT
moderate

**4 soft cottage bread rolls
(or brioche rolls)**

**4 heaping tablespoons
chocolate hazelnut spread**

Set up your barbecue for direct cooking over moderate heat (around 180°C/350°F). A campfire, firepit or barbecue that has died down to embers is an ideal opportunity to make these rolls; you don't want flames, just a gentle heat to warm the rolls through.

Remove the top knot from the cottage rolls, or cut a hole in the top of the brioche rolls.

Use a teaspoon to hollow out a well inside each roll. Fill the well in each roll with a heaping tablespoon of chocolate hazelnut spread and pop the lids back.

Wrap each roll in a double layer of foil and place in the warm embers of the campfire or barbecue for around 10–15 minutes. Make sure the embers are not too hot, or the rolls will burn. You want the rolls to crisp up a little bit and the chocolate spread to be melted and runny.

To serve, unwrap the rolls and enjoy getting as messy as you like.

Unsurprisingly, this is a recipe my kids came up with, and it has become a firm (very sweet) family favourite! It is a riff on the chocolate hazelnut brioche rolls (opposite). It's great to get the kids involved in fire cooking with adult help – with a bit of guidance they will soon feel confident in a skill that will stay with them for life (and there's nothing wrong with a bit of sweet fun at the end of any barbecue meal).

BISCOFF S'MORE ROLLS

FEEDS 2

RECOMMENDED HEAT
low–moderate

2 giant barbecue marshmallows

2 brioche rolls

2 tablespoons Lotus Biscoff (Speculoos spiced cookie spread)

2 long, flat metal skewers

Set up your barbecue for direct cooking at low–moderate heat (around 140–160°C/280–320°F). You can also use a firepit, campfire or barbecue that has died down.

Place a marshmallow on each skewer (these should be long enough to keep little hands away from the heat) and let the kids toast them slowly over the coals until they are soft and lightly browned on the outside.

Toast the brioche buns lightly directly on or over the coals.

Spread 1 tablespoon Biscoff Spread onto the base of each brioche roll.

Place the toasted marshmallow on top of the Biscoff Spread, add the top of the roll and, using the roll to keep the marshmallow in place, withdraw the skewer.

Wrap the whole roll in foil (to keep in the melting Biscoff Spread) and place near the coals to warm up for 4–5 minutes.

Unwrap and enjoy! It's messy, but delicious.

INDEX

ACKNOWLEDGEMENTS

I'm so very fortunate to have the full support and love of my darling wife Lisa, without you by my side I could not do what I do, thank you for being my rock. Thank you to my wonderful children Rory, Elsie and Louie, your feedback and input into my food is always appreciated with love. Seeing you cherish your copies of my books means the world to me. Thank you to my parents, Dad you are my hero, and Mum I miss you. We have so many wonderful bbqs with the Bawdon, Cassidy and Gosley families. To all my dear friends, I am so fortunate to have you in my life. For me, when I cook for you, I am showing you I care for you. Thank yous and big smoky love to all my friends in the global BBQ community. BBQ people are the best people, you love what you do and the world is a better place because you do it. We need positivity now more than ever and BBQ is a shining light. To those who have attended classes at my UK BBQ School in Devon, the more I teach, the more I learn, thank you for your visits. Thank you to my superstar Agent Robert Gwyn Palmer for believing in me, your patience and upbeat enthusiasm keep me going; I love our chats. Thank you so much to the team at RPS for having the vision to see the potential in this book, especially Julia and Sally – you have helped me bring my dreams to fruition. The businesses I work with who support CountryWoodSmoke, the Butchers, BBQ companies, charcoal makers, rub and sauce producers. It's an exciting time for UK BBQ and I am enjoying sharing the ride with you Thank you to Rupert and Kelly, David and the BBQ Mag team, you've taken a digital dream of a BBQ Magazine and turned it into something epic. Thank you to Matt Fowler I love working with you to create awesome content and to Glynn Christian and Dan Toombs, your support and encouragement meant this book happened, without your mentoring and guidance it may not have.

TEMPERATURE CHARTS

ESTIMATING THE COOKING TEMPERATURE

The quickest way to estimate the cooking temperature is to put your hand very carefully around 15 cm/6 inches – conveniently, the height of a soft drinks can – above the cooking surface of your grill. The longer you can hold your hand there, the cooler the cooking temperature. Note: Please do this very carefully – I don't want you burning yourself and getting me into trouble… Here are the number of seconds you will be able to hold your hand above the cooking surface and the temperatures ranges to which these times equate:

Red hot	Less than 2 sec. /instantaneous	350°C (660°F) +
High	2–3 sec.	280–350°C (530–660°F)
Medium hot	4–5 sec.	180–230°C (350–450°F)
Moderate	6–8 sec.	150–180°C (300–350°F)
Low to moderate	9–10 sec.	120–150°C (250–300°F)
Low	11–14 sec.	65–120°C (150–250°F)

INTERNAL TEMPERATURE GUIDE

An internal temperature or temperature range is provided for many recipes. I have suggested what I consider to be the best internal cooking temperature, but feel free to adjust this for meats such as beef and lamb that can be cooked to suit personal taste. But be especially careful to cook poultry and pork products to the stated temperature for food safety.

BEEF / LAMB / VEAL / VENISON

Blue	46–49°C (115–120°F)
Rare	52–55°C (125–130°F)
Medium rare	55–60°C (130–140°F)
Medium	60–65°C (140–150°F)
Medium well	65–69°C (150–155°F)
Well done	71–100°C (160–212°F)

PORK

Medium	63°C (145°F)
Well done	71°C (160°F)

POULTRY

N/A	74°C (165°F)

FISH

N/A	63°C (145°F)